HOUSTON
CULTURE SHOCK

William Dylan Powell

Copyright © 2020 by Reedy Press, LLC
Reedy Press
PO Box 5131
St. Louis, MO 63139, USA
www.reedypress.com

We (the publisher and the author) have done our best to provide the most accurate information available when this book was completed. However, we make no warranty, guarantee, or promise about the accuracy, completeness, or currency of the information provided, and we expressly disclaim all warranties, express or implied. Please note that attractions, company names, addresses, websites, and phone numbers are subject to change or closure, and this is outside of our control. We are not responsible for any loss, damage, injury, or inconvenience that may occur due to the use of this book. When exploring new destinations, please do your homework before you go. You are responsible for your own safety and health when using this book.

Library of Congress Control Number: 2020937343

ISBN: 9781681062778

Design by Jill Halpin

Printed in the United States of America
20 21 22 23 24 5 4 3 2 1

DEDICATION

This book is dedicated to my parents, Bill and Jeanette Powell,
who taught me how to make myself at home
anywhere in the world.

ACKNOWLEDGMENTS

Thanks to Thomas Guerrero and Edgar-nominated author Hector Acosta for the taco tip; to Elizabeth Le Pori Fordham and Trae Stanley on Houston's churches; to Kim G. Lain and Danny Reeves regarding rap; to Cameron Wallace for the reminder to include Jim McIngvale; to Jason Merchant and Greg Barker on including "swangas"; and Jon Feagain for the tip on including the restaurant scene. Also thanks to Chris Conley for his man cave pics. Thank you to the Menil Collection for photo support. Thanks to Janeen Comer regarding the HLSR and Denise Patrick on NASA, TMC, and so on; to my good friend Tor Butterfield for the idea to include HS football—we're overdue for lunch and/or drinks; to Dan Clark (12A!) on including Viet Cajun food; to Liz Poirier regarding Juan Carlos; to Raycheal Proctor for the tip about Houston cycling; and to Justin Galloway on including humidity. Thanks to Temple Walker on including "wards" and to Donna Harvey Collum for the tip on transportation. Thanks to Rachael Porter for a newcomer's perspective. Thanks to Lisa Gray for the reminder to include the multiple clusters of high-rises and Transco; to Misty Clark Loocke and novelist Laura Elvebak for the info on the lack of zoning; to the fast-footed Eric Irvin for the push to include Houston's heat; and to Kathryn Lane for suggesting the HMNS and NASA. Thanks to David Falloure for a nudge to include the arts, and thanks to my college buddy Dane Breitzig for suggesting the lack of basements. Much appreciation goes out to everyone who contributed photos, including Carter Fitts and Tatum Boatwright at the TMC; the Nutcracker Market and Fulton Davenport at PWL Studio; Donna McClendon,

Margaret McKee, and Sarah Hobson at the Menil; Lydia Baehr once again with NMFH help; and everyone at Operation BBQ Relief: Dewayne Daniel, Sharon Green, James Edward Bates, and the Houston Livestock Show and Rodeo. Thanks to Britney Jackson for graffiti advice and a variety of Skittles flavors. Taste the rainbow.

CONTENTS

SECTION 11—LOCAL LEGENDS

INTRODUCTION

I wrote this book primarily for those who have recently moved to town and need to know what to expect as a Newstonian. But it's also for proud native Houstonians and longtimers who are just really into all things H-Town and want to celebrate its flavorful, quirky culture. For those who've just moved here, I'd like to be the first to welcome you and also ask that you please get over in the right-hand lane if you insist on going the speed limit. Watch for potholes.

Moving can be tough. Even when things go well, rather than a "fresh start," what you usually get is fresh stress. You get lost, you have fewer friends, usually you're taking on a new job with new people, and where the #$&! did that one box go? And you don't really know the new place—not just the logistics of it but its soul. You don't know what you're dealing with, unless you move to Manhattan, the soul of which is pretty much just people stealing your cab until you eventually run out of money. But outside of that, there's a lot of stress to moving someplace new—a lot of culture shock.

After you get through all that, though, you can start to appreciate the authentic experiences, attitudes, and opportunities of your new home. That's where I hope *Houston Culture Shock* can help. I have compiled 77 different things to note about Houston life, ranging from weather and wildlife to local legends to treasured events and unique destinations.

There's way, way too much to this city than would fit into one little book like this—natives will recognize the shortcomings—but it's a start. Also, Houston means many things to many people;

it's possible to get "culture shock" moving from Montrose to Katy, much less moving here from the United Kingdom or California.

For native Houstonians, I'm hoping this book is a good way to share the communities and culture they've created. Houston is the kind of place you must experience to appreciate. It's got problems, and no place is perfect, but there really is no other place like it. And it's changing all the time. Well, 290 is probably still under construction. Still, though, it's always changing.

Also, a quick note about the blurred line between Houston and Texas. The two are not always one and the same. In some ways, we have more in common with New Orleans and Atlanta than Dallas or Austin. But Houston is definitely a part of Texas, with its share of Texas pride. So I've included some things that are true in Houston but also other parts of the state, such as our love of Whataburger, iced tea addiction, and the obsession with (mostly unnecessary) pickup trucks. These Texas-centric quirks are shocking if you're from Germany but not so much if you're from Plano. Still, I allowed some overlap.

Lastly, I wrote this book during the COVID-19 lockdown. I did my best with things like photography given everything going on (or not). My priority was keeping people safe and staying out of the way, which was pretty easy for a guy who's been a professional writer for 20 years. We were social distancing way before it was cool.

So kick back with a Topo Chico, and maybe a taco; perhaps catch some fresh air under a shade tree at Memorial Park. Let's dig into this glorious mess of humanity and humidity that is Houston. If you enjoy this book or want to keep up with future projects, follow me on Twitter or Instagram @houstonwriter.

What kind of people live here?

Most Texans know how diverse Houston is, but those who move here from elsewhere are often surprised at the city's diversity. If you haven't been here, all you know is that it's (1) in Texas, and (2) in the South. To the uninitiated, this doesn't scream diversity. But that's pretty, well, prejudiced—a preconceived opinion not based on fact.

The fact is that Houston is all about diversity. In fact, a 2017 *LA Times* article noted that it surpassed New York in 2010 to "become the most racially and ethnically diverse major metropolis in the country."

Its massive growth in recent decades, as well as its relaxed attitudes toward race, immigration, gender, and sexuality, have made Houston what Smithsonian Magazine calls the "Next Great American City," 25 years ahead of the rest of the nation. (Fun fact: The author of that story was robbed at gunpoint while visiting.) I

八號公路

Many of the street signs in Houston's "Chinatown" are in Chinese.

LIFESTYLE & PEOPLE

The first mosque in downtown Houston, the Islamic Da'wah Center was founded by Hakeem Olajuwon.

once had lunch with two coworkers of Mexican American heritage at a Korean restaurant. Neither spoke Spanish, but both spoke passable German and used it to complain to one another about the *bulgogi*. We'll get to food snobbery later, but these kinds of scenes aren't what outsiders envision when they think "Houston." For the record, I thought there was nothing whatsoever wrong with the *bulgogi*.

People come to Houston in search of opportunity, and many find it. In matters of economic equality, this city's not without its issues. But the "H" in H-Town can stand for "home" no matter who you are. Most Houstonians are either too educated, cosmopolitan, or focused on making money to get hung up on labels. We're comfortable all being in the hustle together. So you do you, whatever your cultural heritage and whatever that means. Just stay off your phone when driving.

More than 145 languages are spoken in Houston. It ranks third in the US for number of languages behind NYC (192) and LA (185).

Dallas?
Never heard of it.

Not a big fan of the metroplex

Houston has always had a chip on its shoulder toward its North Texas counterpart, for several reasons. Here are a few.

The 1978 TV show *Dallas* did two extremely annoying things. First, the show's worldwide fame meant Dallas was the only Texas city people had ever heard of. In college, I spent some time studying in London, and everyone I met upon hearing my accent would say: "From Dallas are you, mate? Oi, who shot JR?" No, Simon. I am not from Dallas.

The other thing the TV show did was build the misconception that Dallas was ground zero for the oil business. Both Dallas and Houston have powerhouse economies that outpace the gross domestic product of many nations. But for better or worse, Houston houses around 4,600 energy firms, including 600 exploration and production firms, 1,100 oilfield service providers, and 180 pipeline companies.

And then there are sports: Texans vs. Cowboys, Dynamo vs. Dallas FC, Rockets vs. Mavs. I grew up an Oilers fan, dealing with The Choke in 1993 while the Dallas Cowboys became America's Team. Some Houstonians find Dallas pretentious and materialistic, which is kind of funny considering you can have a Ferrari delivered to your house in Houston. Each sees the other as being a little colloquial and behind the times. And many people in Dallas consider Houston to be dirty and blue collar.

 LIFESTYLE & PEOPLE

Still, Dallas is in Texas. We can trash talk them, but we're also the first to get their back if a New Yorker puts them down. Houstonians will trek up to the State Fair of Texas (since the Houston Livestock Show and Rodeo is over), watch the Red River Rivalry, and join forces in rolling their eyes at Austin.

Of course, if you ask anyone from Dallas, they'll say there's absolutely no rivalry whatsoever because they never even think about us. But, of course, that's exactly what one of those Mary-Kay-selling, big-haired snobs would say, isn't it? Love y'all. Mean it.

The Texans and Cowboys play for the Texas Governor's Cup each year; as of this writing, we've won three straight games.

"Fort Worth hates Dallas. Houston hates Dallas and Austin. San Antonio hates Austin. Austin wishes all the rest of us would just go away, and Dallas pretends that none of the rest of us even exist."
—John Nova Lomax, *Texas Monthly*, August 31, 2015

Where can I find the "In" crowd?

Just as many Londoners don't much care to go south of the river, and Manhattanites often consider "bridge and tunnel" folk to be a primitive and migratory subspecies who've just now mastered fire and toolmaking, many people simply never leave Loop 610.

These Houstonians consider the Inner Loop the center of all action and culture, and where you'll find anything worth finding. Is this true? You'll have to make that call for yourself.

It's not a rivalry, like Dallas vs. Fort Worth or Austin vs. Actual Texas. It's just that Inner Loopers often simply aren't that interested in what goes on around Houston's outskirts. You might ask them how to get to Aldine or Missouri City, and

For many people, when they say "Houston" they actually mean the bit of Houston inside Loop 610.

6

The area inside Loop 610 is around 110 square miles. That's bigger than the entire cities of Charleston, Savannah, Abilene, Tallahassee, or Sacramento.

they might not know any more than someone from Tulsa.

Loop 610 was opened in 1973, the original idea actually being a defensive loop around the city first conceived in 1941 to move troops and materials around town in preparation for World War II. Of course, we didn't much need a defensive perimeter in 1973 Houston, except maybe against disco or cholesterol. But over the coming decades, the loop served as a sort of cultural demarcation line for many.

Inner Loop properties often come at a premium. Nothing is black and white in Houston, so it's not quite accurate to say only people with money live in the loop (there are great real estate deals to be had in Third Ward or Kashmere Gardens, if you don't mind driving a mine-resistant, armor-plated vehicle). But perceived classism and a bit of cultural elitism are definitely part of the Inner Loop mystique for some.

There's also just objective truth, though. The Inner Loop includes some of Houston's most prosperous, interesting, and treasured people and places. The important thing is finding the place that's right for you, inside or outside.

Do people really have guns here?

Trigger warning. Get it? But, seriously, the topic of guns can be a divisive one in today's America. So if you think reading this section will raise your blood pressure, maybe you should just skip it. But if you're curious and have an open mind, this is an interesting and widespread part of H-Town culture.

No matter how you feel about it personally, the fact is that guns have been a part of American culture since the nation's founding—and a cherished part of Texas and Houston culture since the days of the Republic of Texas.

Modern gun ownership is a rite of passage for many Houstonians. Some consider it an essential tool in keeping their family safe, while others shoot competitively or perhaps enjoy getting

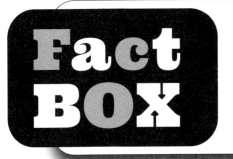

Fact BOX

Think gun ranges are just bro hangouts? Nope. In fact, many Houston ranges have a ladies' night where women can shoot at a discount or even for free.

LIFESTYLE & PEOPLE

8

out of the crowded city to hunt. Whatever their reason for exercising their Second Amendment rights, it's an everyday part of life for many Houstonians.

This being the case, Houstonians often have guns at home or hold a license to carry a handgun on their person. Depending on where they're from, visitors find this either fascinating or terrifying. For Houstonians who host out-of-towners, and especially those from abroad, it's not uncommon for visitors to want to experience what it's like to shoot. And with the proper safety training and environment, there are plenty of places to oblige them.

There are dozens of public gun ranges in the greater Houston area, ranging from upscale experiences such as the Athena Gun Club on the westside to long-standing favorites such as Top Gun and even those serving specific neighborhoods. So if you overhear two housewives debating the merits of Glock vs. 1911 handguns at the grocery store, don't freak out. It's not the apocalypse. It's just Texas.

At Collectors Firearms, you can buy anything from modern sporting rifles to an authentic set of flintlock dueling pistols from the 1800s. Athena Gun Club offers rentals, classes, and the feel of an upscale executive shooting club.

MINIMUM OCTANE RATING
(R + M) / 2 METHOD

87

P R E S S

Yay! High oil prices?

Nobody likes it when their household expenses go up, but the energy industry is still so much of the Houston economy that it's not uncommon to hear people around town rooting for the prices of oil and gas to go up. That's because the financial well-being of so many Houstonians is tied to the oil and gas industry—a fact that's been both a blessing and a curse.

Though there are other major oil and gas centers, such as Dubai, Aberdeen, and Calgary, Houston is widely known as the energy capital of the world.

At the time this was written, more than 237,000 Houstonians worked directly in oil and gas as petroleum engineers, landmen, geologists, executives, traders, and other specialists. We have a higher concentration of engineers than any other major US metropolitan area. Of the nation's 138 publicly traded oil and gas companies, 39 are headquartered here, and the others are shared across the rest of Texas and the nation.

Houston's economy is less dependent on energy than it once was. Still, even if you're not in the industry, the price of oil and gas likely impacts you. Whether you're an attorney specializing in intellectual capital, a surgeon, a graphic designer, a car salesman,

 LIFESTYLE & PEOPLE

or a restaurateur, oil and gas folk do much of the spending in this town. So when oil is up, business is good for everyone— unlike the rest of the country when high oil prices just mean bigger bills.

When oil prices are low, you may actually hear someone complain about it at the pumps. That person may have helped find, produce or refine the crude oil from which that fuel was made.

Another thing most people don't consider is that Houston is also ground zero for lowering global carbon emissions. That's because the technical expertise to make this new "energy transition" happens to come from the same organizations that understand how it works now. Houston companies are at the forefront of carbon-reduction technologies, including carbon sequestration, solar power, biofuels, wind energy, energy efficiency technologies, industrial emissions capture, and more.

In addition to energy, Houston also has the nation's leading US port in terms of waterborne tonnage, the nation's largest medical center, and a huge industrial sector.

How MEGA are your megachurches?

Everything is bigger in Texas, and church is no exception. According to a study by the Hartford Institute for Religious Research, Houston has a whopping 37 "megachurches." They defined a megachurch as "a Protestant congregation that has an average weekly attendance of 2,000 or more."

Photo courtesy of Ian Espinosa on Unsplash.

The combined average weekly attendance at Houston's megachurches would total approximately 640,000 people—a number greater than the population of Atlanta. Churches of this size provide not only spiritual guidance for members but also serve as communities-within-a-community. Here are some of Houston's biggest:

- Lakewood Church 43,500 members
- Second Baptist Church 23,659 members
- The Woodlands Church 16,380 members
- New Light Church 13,500 members
- The Fountain of Praise 9,000 members

With a $90M annual budget, the nondenominational Lakewood Church is by far

 LIFESTYLE & PEOPLE

Lakewood Church was the world's first auditorium church conversion.

Houston's most mega of churches. Lakewood pastor Joel Osteen succeeded his father, John Osteen, as Lakewood's leader more than 20 years ago. Under his stewardship, the church has gone beyond local to include a TV network called Hope TV, live streaming services, global missions, its own app, and more. And scaling up pays; Osteen and his wife live in a 17,000+ square foot River Oaks mansion valued at $12M.

According to a Rice University Kinder Institute Houston area survey, only about 45 percent of Houstonians attended a religious service in the previous month. Around 80 percent of Houstonians considered themselves religious, however. We've also got the nation's second-largest number of Baptist congregations in the United States.

Among Houstonians who profess a non-Christian religion, 28 percent are Jewish, 14 percent are Hindu, 14 percent are Muslim, 14 percent are Buddhist, and the remaining 30 percent comprise all other religions, including, presumably, Jedis and people who worship James Harden's beard. Peace be with you.

The building that hosts Lakewood Church was once an arena called The Summit (later renamed Compaq Center). Metallica, George Strait, Depeche Mode, Rush, and AC/DC all played there. Its capacity was 16,285.

Fact BOX

What's the city's most despised cliché?

Montrose hipsters or westside conservatives. Inner Looper singles or Pearland parents. Aggies or Longhorns. On this issue, we all stand united: the "Houston, we have a problem" cliché must be killed with fire. It's not a witty way to relate to the locals; it's a way to induce involuntary groaning and eye-rolling.

I have personally seen headlines reading:
- Houston, We Have a Job Opening (Space Force)
- Houston, We Have a Craving (Space Cookies)
- Houston, We Have a Recipe (Space Diets)
- Houston, We Have a Weight Problem (OK, I'll give 'em that one)

As I was writing this, a BBC documentary came on called "Houston, We Have a New Criminal Justice System." You can buy T-shirts on Amazon that read "Houston, We Have a Prob-Llama," featuring an astronaut llama in a space helmet. NASA has a podcast called "Houston, We Have a Podcast." You can even buy "Houston, We Have a Baby" birth announcements.

It's not funny, it's not clever, and we don't like it. It's not even accurate.

The phrase had its origins in the Apollo 13 mission—or, more accurately, the portrayal of the Apollo 13 mission in the

 LIFESTYLE & PEOPLE

Fact BOX

There's a Twitter account called @UghHouston that chronicles the latest lame "Houston We Have a Problem" groaner headlines.

Apollo 13 movie starring Tom Hanks, Bill Paxton, Gary Sinise, and Kevin Bacon. In real life, astronaut Jack Swigert, upon learning there was an explosion on the ship that destroyed some of the mission's oxygen supplies, radioed Houston and said: "OK, Houston, we've had a problem here."

In the 1995 Ron Howard film, Tom Hanks, who played Swigert, simply said: "Houston, we have a problem." And just like that, everyone started saying it.

As Lisa Gray of the *Houston Chronicle* lamented in a 2018 article: "It doesn't matter what Houston story makes international news. When the wider world pays attention to us, we know what they're going to say . . . . They'll use *that* phrase: the tagline from the movie *Apollo 13*."

SILENCIO
SILENCE

Don't. Just don't. Photo courtesy of Scott Umstattd on Unsplash.

What's a quinceañera?

If you're new to Houston, you'll soon experience this phenomenon. You're somewhere scenic—the park, a museum, or a fancy hotel. A stretch limo pulls up, and professional photographers appear from nowhere. Suddenly there's a crowd. People dressed to the nines come out of the woodwork. What's happening? Is it some kind of celebrity sighting?

Then the door of the limo pops open and there appears . . . a 15-year-old girl.

A photo shoot commences and then, as quickly as they appeared, the young woman and her entourage are whisked away to some fancy venue, leaving the crowd in awe. You've just seen a quinceañera in progress, and in H-Town, they are a big deal.

A rite of passage in Hispanic cultures, the quinceañera is celebrated when a girl turns 15. It marks her passage from girlhood into womanhood and is both a religious and cultural event widely celebrated in Mexico, Latin America, the Caribbean—and all over H-Town.

Depending on family background and traditions, the specific trappings of the quinceañera can vary a bit. But, generally, it starts with a mass that includes the girl and her family as well as the girl's godparents. Then there's a party. Sometimes a HUGE

 LIFESTYLE & PEOPLE

Rental horse? Dress? Tiara? All at the ranch? Absolutely for those who can spare no expense. Photo courtesy of Laura Gomez on Unsplash.

¿Cuanto cuesta una Quinceañera? A lot. Like weddings, some quinceañeras are very modest and others are quite extravagant. Some families drop $50,000, $100,000 or even more for this special celebration.

Fact BOX

party. The girl appoints a court that includes boys and girls, known as *chambelánes* and *damas*. With girls often in poofy pink dresses and boys in tuxes, there is a DJ, band, or both; elaborate multitiered cakes; speeches; and everything you can imagine that comes with a fancy formal celebration.

Much like the wedding, the quinceañera has created its own industry, with specialized photographers, bakers, planners, florists, venues, and more. Families pack NRG Stadium and the George R. Brown Convention Center to get inspiration on dresses, themes, and the latest trends.

How cold does it get in the winter?

Hot for the holidays

Winters in Houston are mild. Like, really mild. Sure, we have cold snaps, and it snows or freezes on occasion. But, in general, you're more likely to be able to grill steaks than to need a super-heavy coat in the winter. People often say we only get about two weeks of winter each year; that's not exactly true, but consider these Houston winter facts:

- Houston has had only 14 recordable snowfalls since 1939.
- In the average year, Houston has 99 or more days that are over 90 degrees and only 18 days below freezing.
- In December 2016, starting on Christmas Eve, highs were in the 80s for four consecutive days.
- In January 2020, there were no freezing days in Houston.
- I'm writing this on February 29, 2020, and the high today is 75; the bluebonnets are already blooming.

This warm winter messes with people's minds because they're watching Hallmark movies in which adorable people wearing adorable winter wear are making adorable snowmen. Also, every store in town is selling parkas and skiwear despite the fact that you probably can't wear any of that around here without giving yourself heat stroke.

 WEATHER WEIRDNESS

A rare dusting of snow in H-Town a few years ago

Chestnuts? Nah, we're good. We like steak roasting on an open fire. Photo courtesy of Paul Hermann via Unsplash.

As a result, whenever it gets colder than 60 degrees, women throw on their fur coats and fur-lined boots, sweating heavily but looking fashionable. And every fireplace in every neighborhood lights up at once in a mild cool-down, even though they're also running the air conditioners. If the forecast mentions even the most statistically remote possibility of ice or snow, the entire city shuts down and clears out H-E-B shelves as if the apocalypse were coming.

Fact BOX

There's a local rumor that if we have a hurricane in any given year, it will also snow. Is this true? Nah, snow is actually more common. It's just that hurricanes are pretty memorable events.

What's it like during hurricane season?

Hunkering down

Most Houstonians have a hurricane story. The most violent storms on earth, hurricanes form when warm air from waters around the equator rises and, in an attempt to resolve the surrounding pressure differential, ends up creating a big, swirling, banded nightmare of a storm that kills people and breaks things.

People who live in hurricane country ask themselves questions other people might not, such as: "How much drinking water do I have?" and "What's the fastest evacuation route not likely to be gridlocked?" Or "Which of my neighbors can I sleep with in exchange for a generator and window air conditioner?" OK, maybe not the last one. But, still, we try to think ahead.

Officially, hurricane season runs from June 1 to November 30, but most Houston storms happen between mid-August and mid-September. Harvey (2017), Ike (2008), and Rita (2005) were among the recent worst. Hurricanes bring with them high wind, rainfall flooding, storm surge flooding, power outages, and other problems.

Obviously, some of the biggest storms were catastrophic. Harvey alone killed 68 people, spawned 57 tornadoes, and did $120 billion in damage. So they're pretty scary. But they don't happen every day—and there are things Houstonians typically do before, during, and after the storm to minimize the impact on their lives.

 WEATHER WEIRDNESS

Early warning technology has come a long way, so you generally have a week or so to prepare (unlike a tornado or earthquake). And as terrible as Houstonians can be in traffic, we typically pull together to help each other out in a storm. Plus, when they're sure the power is going to be out, many people have neighbors over for a hurricane party because you'd hate for those steaks to go bad anyway—and you could use a cold beer after all of that getting ready.

Dating tip: The home generator is hurricane country's sexiest home accoutrement come storm season.

What's the deal with flooding?

Keeping your head above water

Houston is a huge city close to sea level in a rainy, subtropical coastal climate. That brings with it some cool stuff such as easy gardens and big, lush green spaces. Unfortunately, it also means that nature occasionally tries to reclaim the city in a way that requires us to do everything short of gathering two of every animal onto an oceangoing vessel.

Houston has flooded ever since there's been a Houston. And though devastating flooding happens during hurricanes such as Harvey, there doesn't need to be a named storm for the city to flood. There doesn't even need to be a particularly large storm. Flooding has impacted almost all Houstonians, whether they've lost a home or were just forced to take "flood days" from work or school. Flood days are our snow days down here.

Never drive into ponded water on the roadway when you can't tell how deep it is. Not only do people die like that, but you can ruin your vehicle instantly.

Fact BOX

WEATHER WEIRDNESS

Beltway 8 held an astonishing 16+ feet worth of water during Hurricane Harvey.

Why does Houston flood so much?

It's a combination of things. For openers, it's just a flat place that gets a lot of rain—more rain than Seattle. The city is just barely above sea level and sports clay soil that saturates quickly. In addition, we have huge urban sprawl, and this widespread development has meant the loss of natural wetland and prairie land. Paved land actually generates five times more runoff than natural habitats, and we've got plenty of pavement. Oh, and some of Houston is sinking.

So yeah, there are lots of reasons.

As a result, there are things Houstonians should do to play it safe. Before you buy or rent, check the property's flood history. But also understand that just because it hasn't happened doesn't mean it couldn't. Despite the melodrama, watch the forecast. Always check in on the elderly and others who might not be able to help themselves. And avoid driving when it's potentially unsafe or messing around in floodwaters if you can help it.

Why is my car yellow?

Pollen the family

One great thing about Houston is that despite the population, it's still lush and verdant, with trees everywhere and lots of parkland. In fact, the Houston park system spans more than 38,000 acres. But all of that green space comes at a price when it comes to allergies.

Not everybody suffers from allergies, but if you're susceptible, Houston is a house of respiratory horrors. Allergies occur when you breathe in tree pollen or mold, and your body identifies it as a foreign substance—resulting in a runny nose, sneezing, puffy eyes, and the desire to take a chain saw to every tree within a 20-mile radius.

One reason allergy season can be a pain here is that it's not a one-and-done affair; we actually have three different allergy seasons. Allergies first spike up in January when trees start flowering; it's crazy to watch yellow clouds of pollen fall out of the trees all over town. As spring transitions to summer, grass pollen kicks off. Then in early fall it's ragweed season. In addition, our warm and wet climate means a natural outdoor mold count, including things like *Alternaria, Aspergillus, Cladosporium,* and a bunch of other stuff it sounds like you might buy at Whole Foods.

So between three different allergy seasons, it can definitely feel like a sustained attack. Some days your freshly washed car will be covered in yellow. But all that said, Houston isn't the worst place

 WEATHER WEIRDNESS

for allergies. In fact, one recent poll by the Asthma and Allergy Foundation of America ranked Houston at #56 for spring allergy capitals; #1 was McAllen, Texas.

Houstonians susceptible to allergies just need to check the pollen and mold count the same way many people check the weather for the next day—adjusting their plans and meds accordingly. Bless you.

Who likes oak pollen season? Car washes, that's who.

The trick to staying on top of allergies? Assuming your doc OKs medicine, take your allergy meds first thing in the morning before you get out in the thick of things.

Fact BOX

What's worse: Humidity or Houmidity?

Unless they moved here from Vietnam, or the inside of a golden lab's mouth, newcomers to Houston might notice Houston's muggy, humid air. Houston has an average humidity of 78 percent, ranking as the ninth most humid city in the United States.

To put that in perspective, a humidor is what cigar smokers keep their cigars in so they don't dry out (the cigars, not the smokers—many cigar smokers will never dry out). The optimal humidity setting for a humidor is between 70 and 75 percent. So, yep, the average Houston humidity is too humid for a humidor. Vietnam actually shares the same humidity averages. Around six in the morning, Houston's humidity often reaches around 90 percent.

When you hear people express atmospheric humidity in a percentage, they mean the relative humidity, which is a ratio of the current absolute humidity to the highest possible absolute humidity. A relative humidity of 100 percent means that the air can't physically hold any more water at a given temperature. This doesn't necessarily mean that it's raining, but it probably does mean your hair looks as though you've commuted to work via triathlon.

Humidity can often feel gross because very humid air interferes with the ability of our sweat to evaporate. It's a good idea to

 WEATHER WEIRDNESS

Fact BOX

Houston humidity can reach 100 percent, but that doesn't always mean rain. Rain happens when saturation occurs in the clouds rather than ground level, where it becomes fog and dew.

drink more water in humid places, especially if you're an athlete. To compensate for this inefficient evaporation, your body sweats more in humid conditions. Interestingly, people's sense of smell is heightened in more humid air, which is a mixed blessing depending on whether you're driving by a bakery or a refinery. Butterflies love Houston's humid air; butterfly houses are often kept at around 78 percent humidity.

When you're getting ready, give yourself a few extra weeks to dry your hair. Photo courtesy of Arun Sharma via Unsplash.

Is ZONING really not a thing here?

There's a patch of Westheimer not far from my house that has two churches, a warehouse liquor store, two spas, a Halal meat market, a FedEx, a Luby's, a bank, a Lowe's, an Asian massage parlor, three beauty salons, a wedding venue, a kidney specialist, a dentist, a Chick-fil-A, and a pleasant little Mediterranean cafe. All of this catty-corner to an exclusive gated country club community. Oh, I forgot to mention the WalMart, and the elementary school around the corner, and the boutique health food grocery store.

So . . . what exactly was the plan here? The answer, of course, is that there wasn't a plan at all. Houston has a reputation for a *laissez-faire* attitude toward development. Traditionally a stronghold of capitalism and minimal government interference, Houston is well known for its long-standing rejection of the "Z word."

Zoning in US cities began a little after 1910. It's basically an umbrella term for the local government being able to tell you what

Fact BOX

Wait, the city has a Planning Committee? Of course. This is the nation's fourth-largest city—not Mad Max Beyond Thunderdome. The Houston Planning Commission is a 26-member board appointed by the mayor. It meets every other Thursday.

you can do or build and where. The idea was meant to protect homeowners' property values from devaluation via undesirable nearby development. But of course, that's a slippery slope. Who's to say what's undesirable? This opens up a messy Pandora's box of economic, social, and legal questions.

Rather than heavy-handed, one-size-fits-all regulations, Houston planners instead gradually worked with citizens to create a patchwork of guidelines over time whereby most people could generally do what they wanted. These guidelines cover historic preservation districts, special commercial zones, private deed restrictions, planned communities within Houston, and a number of city ordinances. Anyone who's built a home or business here knows there are plenty of regulations to go around. But it's a more flexible way to do things, pushing decisions closer to landowners rather than bureaucrats.

In this westside shopping center, you can visit the dentist, groom your dog, take a kickboxing class, and get an insurance check-up.

How many
S K Y L I N E S
does Houston have?

If you're from Shanghai or London, the Houston skyline likely won't seem all that remarkable. In fact, the city can seem downright quaint to people coming from huge, global capital cities—offering tons of green space and single-family home development. But one thing that can be confusing to newcomers is that Houston has more than one skyline.

My wife is from Fort Worth. When she first moved here, she would point to a cluster of buildings and say: "Is that downtown?"

"Nope," I'd say. "Galleria."

After a while she'd say. "Oh. I see it over there."

"Nope. That's the Texas Medical Center."

These days she tells me where to go, around town and just in general, but I can see why she was confused.

Downtown is clearly the biggest cluster of tall buildings. But Houston actually has two other big-ish skylines: the Texas Medical Center and the Galleria. The Galleria area's Transc. . . er . . . Williams Tower is 64 stories, so it certainly looks like it should be in a downtown somewhere. And of the 60+ buildings in the Med

According to the Downtown District, you could fit New York, Washington, Boston, San Francisco, Seattle, Minneapolis, and Miami inside the city of Houston. Photo courtesy of Tatiana Rodriguez via Unsplash.

CITYSCAPE

Houston's Uptown looks like many smaller cities' downtown. Make sure to check out the holiday lights around Uptown and Post Oak close to Christmas.

Center, at least 10 of the buildings are more than 20 stories. There are also a few other notable clusters of buildings that catch a bit of sky and give off a downtown-like feel such as the Energy Corridor, CityCentre, Greenway Plaza, and arguably a few others too.

What's Houston's tallest building? That would be the JP Morgan Chase Tower at 600 Travis. Designed by I. M. Pei, it stands at 75 stories and 1,049 feet tall.

You feeling OK?

Nobody wants to get sick. But, hey, if it's going to happen, Houston is a great place for it. Why? The Texas Medical Center.

The Med Center is a city within a city. More than 106,000 people work there, which is more than the entire population of Tyler, Texas. Forty-four of the most prestigious Texas medical institutions have a presence there, including Baylor College of Medicine, Memorial Hermann, Rice University, UT Health, DePelchin's Children's Center, and more.

The Med Center got its start when two things came together fortuitously. First, wealthy Houston banker Monroe Dunaway Anderson left $19M to a foundation upon his death in 1939. Shortly thereafter, the Texas Legislature authorized the University of Texas to establish a cancer research hospital anywhere in Texas. They had a $500,000 budget. The MDA Foundation agreed to match this amount if they built it in Houston. With this modest start, the TMC was born.

The MD Anderson Cancer Center is still, of course, a mainstay. One of the world's best hospitals, it treated more than 146,000 in 2018 alone. Six years ago, it saved my own life. Initially I was told that the non-Hodgkin Lymphoma I had meant a 50-50 chance of living five more years. Today I'm in total remission, which is surely in part luck but also a result of some of the best medical care money can buy.

Original Texas Medical Center concept art from 1940. Photo courtesy of the Texas Medical Center.

CITYSCAPE

And outside of MDA, the scale of it all is just staggering. Taken altogether, the buildings comprising the TMC total 50,000,000 square feet. Ten million patient visits happen there per year, as do 750,000 ER visits and more than 13,500 heart surgeries. More than 25,000 babies are delivered there each year, some of whom are bound to grow up to be doctors who work there.

The Cullens and Andersons at Hermann Hospital on its opening day of 1925. Photo courtesy of the Texas Medical Center.

Fact BOX

Finding a parking space in the Med Center can be a painful procedure all its own. Consequently, many TMC institutions are building satellite offices around town and in the suburbs.

What the #&*! is a ward?

Newcomers not from places such as New Orleans or Newark may notice different parts of town being referred to as "wards" and wonder what that's all about. Houston actually has six wards, each a reference to a bygone system of city government and administration—but still a meaningful community reference.

The ward system was the precursor of today's contemporary city council structure. At one point in US history, peaking in the 1800s, many of the largest cities in the nation divided themselves into wards—each of which had its own leader known as an alderman. The word alderman comes from the Old English *aldormonn*, or a man of high rank, and stood as the title of an official in Anglo-Saxon England who ruled over a shire. Aldermen were elected officials who both lived in the community and provided leadership. The original idea in US politics was to decentralize city leadership so that the mayor didn't accumulate too much power.

In 1905, a number of problems around the city drove its leadership to abolish the ward system for the commission-based government we have today. But the six wards as community identifiers never died. First, Sixth and Fourth Ward are west of downtown going north to south. Third Ward is around Texas Southern University and the University of Houston. Fifth Ward is northeast of downtown, and Fourth Ward is to the south of

Allen Parkway west of Interstate 45. Second Ward is to the southeast of downtown, around the original Ninfa's restaurant on Navigation. Each of these neighborhoods carries its own distinct history and identity.

First Ward was established in 1840 and today sports a thriving arts district.

Old Sixth Ward was listed in the National Register of Historic Places in 1978.

Fact BOX

Possibly the largest concentration of working artists in Texas, the First Ward transformed from a gritty industrial district to the vibrant home of Sawyer Yards—an eclectic collection of art studios.

What's that spotlight in the sky?

Many newcomers to Houston wonder what that enormous lighthouse-like beacon is shining from the Galleria area. Answer? The light atop the Williams Tower.

At 2800 Post Oak, the Williams Tower is 64 stories tall with an imposing arched granite entrance, easy helicopter pad access, and frequent art exhibitions. It's generally seen as a status symbol to have an office in the space. The building was actually designed like two 32-story buildings stacked one on top of the other, complete with two lobbies. Renowned architects Philip Johnson and John Burgee led the project.

The rotating spotlight atop the tower is a comforting landmark for many Houstonians and a handy way to orient yourself within the city. The beacon uses a 7,000 watt light bulb. These massive specialty bulbs need changing every month and cost around $9,000 each. Presumably you can't buy them at IKEA.

Many Houstonians still refer to the building by its original name, the Transco Tower. The name changed in 1998 when its flagship tenant, Transco Energy, was acquired by the Williams Companies. Transco is a pipeline system that starts just west of Corpus Christi and runs to New York City. So Texas plays a role in

 CITYSCAPE

The Transco Tower is the tallest American building outside of a downtown center.

powering up the Broadway Lights, heating the Empire State Building, and letting 21 Club make its famous flaming bananas foster.

The Williams Tower is the tallest American building outside of a downtown area, but post-9/11, you can't just go up to the top of the building and check out the view. There is no observation deck open to the public. A Hines real estate rep told *Houston Chronicle* writer Craig Hlavaty in 2017 that "On a clear day you can see past The Woodlands." The Woodlands, a suburb to the north, is a 40-minute drive from the building in light traffic.

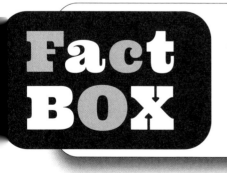

Fact BOX

Houston has 74 licensed heliports within the city proper. But most aren't available for use by the general public and are dedicated to specific corporations, hospital systems, and government institutions.

Do y'all do Taco Tuesday?

Every day in Houston is Taco Tuesday

Religion. Politics. Sports allegiances. Houstonians are generally pretty chill and tolerant with each other regardless of their personal differences. But put your hands up and prepare to duke it out to the death when you share your opinion about who has the best tacos in town because Houstonians have very strong opinions about tacos.

First of all, there are a lot of tacos flying around H-town—and a lot of different places to get them, from taquerias to taco trucks to fancy sit-down places. Everybody has their favorites—Brothers Taco House, Taqueria Arandas, El Tiempo, Gerardo's Drive In, El Taconazo, La Macro, Tacos La Bala, Taquería Don Tin, Xochi, La Calle, Tacos A Go Go, La Tapatia, La Guadalupana—and someone is talking about all of these or dozens of others right now as you're reading this.

There is also someone having a taco-related argument, explaining why whatever taco you love isn't really the best and how you should try this other place for more legit awesomeness. You can love places such as Velvet Taco and Torchy's and tell all of your Houston friends. Just be prepared to listen to them dismiss your faves as over-priced, over-stuffed hipster tacos from Dallas and Austin. For the record, I like Velvet Taco even though

 THE FOOD SCENE

I know it's from Dallas;
fight me. At this point, my
body is around 74 percent
Spicy Tikka Chicken.

The idea of "Taco
Tuesday" was first
registered as a trademark
in 1989 by a Wyoming-
based fast-food franchise
called Taco John's, which
knows better than to
bother opening up a
location in Houston.
But pretty much every
day in Houston is Taco
Tuesday. With hundreds
of taquerias around town,
you'll just have to find
your favorite—and be
prepared to defend them.

Spicy tikka chicken and ahi poke tacos from Velvet Taco.

Fact BOX

Because eating tacos at restaurants, taquerias, taco trucks, and home is not enough, there are also taco-themed events each year, including Tacolandia, Tacoworld!, Tacos X Tequila, and more.

Can I get a refill when you get a chance?

Y'all, we drink so much iced tea down here. If you moved to Houston from somewhere else in Texas or other parts of the South, this won't seem weird. But if you're from anywhere else, you'll be amazed how ever-present iced tea can be in H-Town. It's sold in practically every restaurant, made in most people's homes, served at barbecues and weddings and business meetings, and offered just about anywhere Houstonians congregate.

I'm surprised that when two people have a fender-bender and are exchanging information on the shoulder of the Katy Freeway, someone doesn't just step out of the oleander bushes and say: "Can I refill that tea for you guys?"

Americans in general drink a lot of tea. In 2018, we drank 3.8 billion gallons of the stuff—with 75 to 80 percent of it iced. The South and the Northeast are the nation's biggest tea drinkers; and down here we generally like it iced.

 THE FOOD SCENE

Contrary to popular belief, not everyone in Texas likes sweet tea. Sweet tea is made by adding sugar or simple syrup to the tea while it's still hot, rather than just pouring a packet of sugar into unsweetened tea. The line is blurry, but you'll most often find sweet tea drinkers in parts of Texas that resemble the cultural South such as East Texas—or in families that come from the South. And, well, some people just like sweet tea and don't need a reason. Most Houston restaurants offer both.

Fun fact: June 10 is National Iced Tea Day.

Sure, you can find any type of tea in Houston. Hit Phoenicia and you'll find all of your British loose leaf and favorites from Sri Lanka, India, or the Middle East. The Asian markets will have the finest from China, Thailand, Vietnam, Japan, and so on. There's no shortage of bubble tea spots or specialty stores such as Teavana. But plain old iced tea is everywhere.

Fact BOX

Feeling adventurous? Check out the natural organic selection at Tea Sip in the Heights. For Newstonians, a "Tea Sip" is a left-handed reference to someone who attended UT Austin.

When is crawfish season?

When people think crawfish, they think Louisiana. But when crawfish season rolls around, which is traditionally March and April around here, H-Town has full-blown mudbug fever. In fact, the season is pretty hard to miss. Friends, family and companies organize crawfish boils, popular crawfish restaurants light up, and boiling pots of crawlers even appear in front of the grocery store so you can pick up a few pounds on your way out.

Oilfield workers likely first brought their love of crawfish to Houston from coastal cities such as Port Arthur and Beaumont. The craze caught fire in the 1970s and 1980s, and today some experts say Greater Houston consumes more crawfish than the whole of Louisiana. This seems a ridiculous notion but is actually conceivable since Louisiana has around 4.66 million people according to the 2018 census, and the Greater Houston area is on target to reach 7.1 million in 2020. And, of course, there is no shortage of Louisiana natives in town. Just wait until college

Fact BOX

Crawfish have straight tails that stick out behind them. When they're cooked, the tails curl upward. The exception? If the crawfish is already dead when cooked. These taste awful, so throw them away.

 THE FOOD SCENE

football season rolls around and count the LSU flags in front of people's homes.

Crawfish are sold by the pound. A pound looks like a lot, but crawfish are really just micro-lobsters without a whole lot of meat. Most people eat between one and three pounds in a sitting, but people who really love them can easily eat twice that. Of course, there are many Texans who'd rather eat one to three pounds of dirt than put a crawfish in their mouth. It can be an acquired taste.

Eating crawfish isn't just about the food, though. The slow, social art of prepping, seasoning, boiling, watching, serving, peeling, and eating crawfish is really just about spending time catching up with friends and family—and maybe making some new friends along the way—plus, cold beer.

LA Crawfish has locations all over town for when you crave the mudbugs.

What's the deal with FOOD TRUCKS?

Every major city in the United States has food trucks, but not all food trucks are created equal. It's not the number of food trucks in town that makes Houston's mobile restaurants remarkable; there are only probably around 50 worthy of note. It's the quality that makes them great—and the popularity. From the Filipino street eats of Flip 'N Patties to the cult favorite Oh My Gogi! (OMG) bulgogi truck, people drive all around town to find their favorites.

Restaurateurs often use food trucks to prove out new concepts or launch in a way that keeps a cap on overhead, so many of these trucks are a great way to sample the foods from some of Houston's latest upcoming hot spots. That said, some will be forever mobile—popping up overnight someplace new like mysterious culinary flash mobs.

Houston restaurants such as Mico's Red Hot Chicken, German joint Sauerkraut Grill, gourmet hot dog spot Good Dog, the Rice Box, and many others all started as food trucks first. Los Angeles claims ground zero for the rise in contemporary food trucks in the United States, though the concept goes back to the

 THE FOOD SCENE

Old West chuck wagon and even pre–Revolutionary War street vendors in what is now New York.

Right now, some of the most popular include Eatsie Boys, Pak-Man, The Waffle Bus, Monster PBJ, Muiishi Makirritos, Sticky's Chicken, The DoughCone, Fork & Truck, Coreanos fusion of Korean/Mexican, and Bernie's Burger Bus (don't miss their milkshakes). And if you want to tap in, you'd better stay on your toes. Waze or Google Maps might help, but you're just as likely to be guided to the spot they used to be. Your best bet is to follow your favorite on social media for their latest location or try a food truck app.

Twisted Grilled Cheese offers a number of awesome grilled cheese sammiches, including the 5 Cheese Classic, the 5 Cheese Pepperoni Pizza, a Smokehouse Brisket, Halal Philly Grilled Cheesesteak, and more.

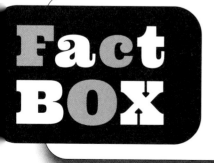

Fact BOX

Not every food truck serves froufrou fusion cuisine catering to hipsters. Don't forget the good old-fashioned taco trucks running around town selling amazing tacos for cheap to hard-working Houstonians.

How about a
cold one?

Houstonians have always loved beer, whether just trying to beat the heat or kicking back from a hard day's work. You can buy beer from anywhere in the world here, but H-Town also sports a number of hometown breweries offering a vast selection of top-quality beers.

Our brewing traditions go back to the 1800s, fueled by Belgian and German immigrants to Houston who knew their trade and moved here to make it big. By 1893, the Houston Ice & Brewing Company occupied a complex of 10 buildings downtown stretching across the bayou. One of its buildings, at 715 Franklin Street, is still standing. Under brand names such as Magnolia, the complex put out award-winning beers that included Southern Select, Richelieu, Grand Prize, and Hiawatha.

Prohibition did them in eventually, but today there are around a dozen serious craft breweries in town, ranging from huge operations to the small-scale and experimental. Texas's oldest craft brewery, Saint Arnold Brewing Company, calls Houston home. With year-round popular beers such as Fancy Lawnmower, as well as seasonal favorites such as its Christmas Ale, almost anyone who loves beer in Houston loves Saint Arnold. And with a full-service beer garden, it's a lot of fun to visit.

EaDo's 8th Wonder Brewery has taken H-Town by storm in recent years with favorites such as its Dome Fauxm, a recreation

THE FOOD SCENE

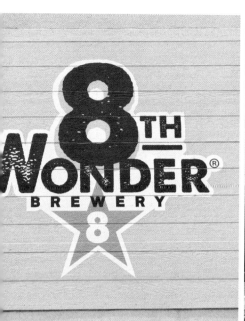

Left: 8th Wonder Brewery (@8thWonderBrew) has a list of refreshing beers as long as a Deshaun Watson pass, as well as a sweet taproom, a distillery, and outsized art from David Adickes. Right: Buffalo Bayou Brewing Company (@Buffbrew) not only has a long list of craft beers but also live music, full-service dining, and a great open-air upstairs patio.

of the beer served at the Astrodome, Weisstheimer hefeweizen, Brewston Texas Pale Ale, and Haterade gose. The 8th Wonder Tap Room is always packed (bring a credit card, no cash), and they have a distillery across the street if beer isn't your thing. Also check out the Buffalo Bayou Brewing Company and its amazing Buff Brew location near Sawyer Yards, as well as Spindletap, Brash Brewing, B-52 Brewing Company, BAKFISH Brewing, Platypus Brewing, and others.

Fact BOX

Want to sample lots of suds and save? The Houston Brew Pass gets you great deals on beer at multiple breweries around town. Google it. Buy it. Drink it.

Whatabrand, huh?

Houstonians have mucho burger options: upscale joints such as Hop Daddy, old school grills such as Stanton's City Bites or Southwell's Hamburger Grill, or outside-of-the-box places such as the buffalo burgers at Bubba's Burger Shack or the Pre-Schooler sliders at Bernie's Burger Bus. But when you're stuck for time and we're talking fast food—it's Whataburger or nothing.

Many kids grew up wanting "water burger" rather than McDonald's. People buy Whataburger stickers, cups, t-shirts, and other merch. We pass up national brands to buy Whataburger ketchup. In 2001, the Texas House and Senate passed a joint resolution making Whataburger a "Texas treasure." Politicians looking to "Texan up" their image leverage Whataburger photo opps. Fans have planted Whataburger flags on mountaintops and brought its cookies into space.

What's with the obsession? First, Whataburger is homegrown in Texas. And if there's anything Texans love it's Texan things. The company's first little stand opened

 THE FOOD SCENE

What's more Texan than iced tea? Iced tea in a Whataburger cup.

on Ayers Street in Corpus Christi. They had 20 restaurants under the company's belt before expanding to other states. Fast food is often seen as soulless and corporate, so having a down-home choice is something we can get behind. So to many, it's not really about the burger at all, but Texas pride.

Houston positively flipped out when the company sold to a Chicago investment bank in 2019; Houston Texans Defensive End J. J. Watt urged Houstonians to chip in and buy it back. Still, its Texas street cred remains more or less intact for most.

Also, they're just good. By design, they've always been bigger than competitors' burgers, and it's a great burger for cheap. They make burgers the way Texans typically like them—meaty, mustardy, and with all kinds of optional jalapeno-laced accoutrements—all made however you want (reportedly 36,000+ combinations).

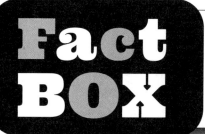

Fact BOX

Whatawedding! Yep, that's right. Vivien Ngyuen and Colton Jung tied the knot at a West Houston Whataburger as part of a contest, exchanging, what else, onion rings.

Are we there yet?

Do yourself a favor and allow plenty of time to get where you need to go. Houston is bigger than most cities—bigger than Boston, bigger than Dallas, and way, way bigger than San Francisco. It's around 669 square miles; that's just Houston proper and not the suburbs. We're talking about more than twice the size of NYC's five boroughs put together. Beltway 8, which loops around most of the city, is 88 miles long. The Grand Parkway (SH 99), a road partially connecting many of Houston's suburbs, has a proposed completed length of 180 miles.

So to put this into perspective, if you're from Philly, driving from one side of Beltway 8 to the other will probably take slightly longer than driving from downtown Philadelphia to Trenton, New Jersey. If you're from London, Houston may seem small population-wise, but we've got a lot of space. Driving the completed Grand Parkway in its entirety would be like driving from Wolverhampton to Brighton.

Fact BOX

When people say "Greater Houston," they could mean any of nine counties that run from The Woodlands down to Galveston and a little further south to places such as Pearland/Alvin.

GETTING AROUND

And then there's the traffic, which ranks as the worst in Texas—but a not-so-bad 11th nationally and 49th in terms of global cities. The average Houstonian spends 81 hours per year sitting in traffic. On the upside, that means usually being in the air conditioning and with plenty of time for Audible or local podcasts. In addition, much like Los Angeles, Houston is the kind of place where you really need a car. Public transportation exists in theory, but it's slow, unreliable, and probably not designed to get you where you need to go.

The average Houston commute is 24 miles roundtrip, the second most expensive commute in the nation.

So if you live in, say, Clear Lake, and you're dating someone from the Richmond/Rosenberg area, I'm not saying you can't make it work. But I am saying you'd better be in love.

Why does my accountant drive a Ford F-350?

Houstonians and trucks: A love story

In most of the world, people drive pickups because there is some technical or logistical requirement for which a normal passenger vehicle just won't do. In Houston? Well, we just like trucks. I mean, sure, there are oil and gas bigwigs with Lamborghinis, business people with Audis, carbon warriors who drive Teslas and Priuses—the usual global cast of auto characters in any other metropolis. But there is a disproportionate love of pickups here that most visitors can't help but remark upon.

The best-selling vehicle in Houston, a city where 30 minutes is considered a not-so-bad commute, is the full-size Ford F-150 pickup truck. Around 16,000 of them were sold in town during 2018 alone. Sometimes, either by happenstance or demographics, parking lots will resemble used truck lots. This enthusiasm even extends to the black market, with the full-size Chevy pickup reigning as the No. 1 stolen vehicle in town. Texans, in general, buy one out of every six full-size pickup trucks made.

This would make sense if we all lived in Levelland and worked on a ranch. But in Houston? Why? The reason is mostly cultural. For one thing, the state's rural heritage makes pickup trucks a Texas tradition. Sure, you might be a corporate bean counter by day, but maybe you're still a cowboy or cowgirl at

 **GETTING AROUND**

heart. There's a certain machismo about them that attracts some. And while they're usually more expensive than standard passenger cars, they're also great for hauling kids, mulch, DIY supplies, furniture, COSTCO groceries and other stuff an urban dweller might need to move around.

Surgeon? Truck. Financial advisor? Truck. Writer of lighthearted books about Houston? Yup. Now there is absolutely no logical reason for any of these people to own a truck, and yet we do it anyway—because Houston.

This is not a used truck lot. This is a Houston Astros game.

What's the BIG DEAL about Buc-ee's?

For Houstonians, it's Buc-ee's or just hold it

They have convenience stores everywhere. But for Houstonians, and most Texans, there can be only one No. 1, so to speak: Buc-ee's. In fact, calling Buc-ee's a convenience store is like calling a mint condition 1966 Corvette Stingray a motor vehicle. It's not wrong, but doesn't come close to doing it justice.

Promising ultra-clean bathrooms, Buc-ee's is a chain of enormous roadside convenience stores. They have the energy of a busy airport, the munchies of a solid Texas roadside fast-food joint, the knickknacks of a roadside gift shop, seemingly bottomless ice, and some of the best coffee on the road. These places can be huge; the Katy location has 120 fuel pumps. Its car wash is the longest automated car wash in the world, as verified by the *Guinness Book of World Records*. And the bathrooms ARE clean, without fail.

Much like Whataburger, Buc-ee's is one of those homegrown Texas brands people will defend to the death. The business was founded by Arch Alpin III and Don Wasek in the small town of Lake Jackson just north of Houston. Big rigs are not allowed on the property, and there are designated places to let your dog go to the bathroom. Through shrewd strategy, brand building, and

 **GETTING AROUND**

knowing their customers, the two turned one location into an empire. There are more than 40 Buc-ee's locations and counting, and the chain recently expanded outside Texas.

Buc-ee's does to the typical convenience store experience what flying private does to the experience of commercial flight: makes the alternative unpalatable. Since its founding, it's redefined the expectations of a roadside convenience store in Texas, so much so that many Houstonians plan their stops on the way to Austin, San Antonio, and Dallas based on which Buc-ee's they'll stop at along the way.

When it comes to roadside bathrooms, gas, munchies, and shopping, there is simply no substitute for the beaver.

What's with the Beaver? Buc-ee's co-founder Arch Alpin III earned the moniker of "Beaver" from his mom when he was a child, and the nickname stuck. Your boy done good, ma'am.

Fact BOX

What are SLABs and Swangas?

If you ask most Texans if they've seen a nice SLAB lately, you may get a description of the most recent smoked brisket they've prepared—or maybe even just a quizzical look. But Houstonians know this distinctive style of African American custom car that was born in H-Town and has spread throughout Texas and the rest of the South.

SLAB is an acronym that stands for slow, loud, and bangin'. These are old-school, large-frame American cars—think Lincoln Town Cars, four-door Cadillacs, Buicks, Oldsmobiles, and the like. These cars actually do look like slabs, which makes the acronym a perfect fit. But these sweet rides are meticulously transformed into something special through candy gloss paint, insane trunk-filling sound systems that can punch holes in the space-time continuum, trunks with light-up messages written on the inside, TVs, gull-wing doors, sick custom vinyl, and more.

And then there's the vehicle's most distinctive feature: "Swangas." If you've driven around Houston, you've

This cherry drop-top was showing off its swangas at the Houston Art Car Festival.

These wire wheels can cost up to $4,000, not counting spares.

likely seen Swangas—elbow wire wheels that stick waaayyy out in the center. They're shiny and eccentric and sport 30 spokes, sometimes with little caps or spinners on the end. They're usually wrapped in whitewalls. They stick out so far that those driving around them feel as though these far-out wheels will dig into their own like one of the battle chariots in the 1959 Charlton Heston film *Ben Hur*.

The love of SLABs and Swangas has grown into a die-hard subculture, and you'll find events all over town where people sport their rides. These can be big, formal affairs such as the Houston Auto Show at NRG Stadium or the Art Car Parade, or just an impromptu affair in a parking lot somewhere. Folks just pull in, pop their trunks, set up lawn chairs, crank music and share these works of art that are distinctly Houston.

Are you saying "Kerr-Ken-Doll"?

Odd Houston pronunciations

Texas is known for not pronouncing things in the way you'd expect—such as calling a city spelled "Refugio," "Refurio," or calling Ruidoso, New Mexico, "Riadosa." And Houstonians are no exception. Check out the actual popular pronunciation of these Houston places and roads around town:

- Bissonnet Street: [biss-o-net], like bassinet (not biss-oh-nay)
- Chenevert Street: [CHEN-uh-vert], not like you'd pronounce it in French
- Duchesne: Catholic all-girls academy is pronounced [doo-SHEN]
- Elgin: Also known as Eastheimer, this road is pronounced [EL-jin], like a glass of gin
- Fuqua: Near William P. Hobby Airport, this road is pronounced [FYOO-kway]
- Houston: Can be [HYOO-stun] or [YEW-stun], but never [HOW-stun] like in Manhattan
- Humble: Pronounced [umble]; their "H" is silent, just like their weekends
- Kuykendahl: Northside road is pronounced [KER-ken-dahl], even though there's no "R"
- Marfreless: River Oaks area speakeasy/smoochie-bar is pronounced [mar-FRAY-less]

 **GETTING AROUND**

- Pecan: Like all cities in Texas, this is a [puh-KAHN] and not a [PEE-can]
- San Felipe: Yep, some actually call this street [san-FIL-uh-pee]
- Schlumberger: Oilfield service giant is pronounced [SHLUM-bur-zhay]
- Synott: Westside road actually pronounced just like "senate"
- Whataburger: Is, in fact, not actually "water-burger" unless you're six years old

Some say Kuykendahl Road was named after a man who allegedly committed a murder and was subsequently hung from the bridge over Cypress Creek.

Clearly that should be pronounced "Kie-ken-dahl," or something, but, no. In Houston, it's "Ker-ken-dahl."

Is that within walking distance?

No—if you have a choice, get a car

Much like Los Angeles, Houston is a good place to have a car. There's no shame in biking or walking everywhere, every day—in fact, if you can make it work you'll be healthier. But most people find this either impractical or unpleasant, and they end up getting a car pretty quick if they have the means.

Houston does have a public transportation system, but, for a city this size, and I'm gonna keep it real here, it's not great. Light rail infrastructure is so small and inconvenient as to be forgettable, unless you work at the Texas Medical Center or are actually struck by a railcar. Public buses are unreliable, not super clean, and take a long time to get you where you're going. And the heat means that walking even three blocks to work in a suit means you'll show up to work smelling like a teenage opossum at least nine months out of the year.

How long would it take to walk across the Houston area? Walking from Katy to Clear Lake would take more than 16.5 hours if you did not stop at all. And your odds of actually making it? Not 100 percent.

Fact BOX

GETTING AROUND

Want an excuse to buy a sweet, sweet car? Just tell your spouse "But I'll be spending so much time commuting. . . ." Photo courtesy of Noah Baughman via Unsplash.

In addition, Houston is pretty spread out. The Houston Metropolitan Statistical Area covers 9,444 square miles—an area larger than five different states. They do actually have shuttles that go from the suburbs to downtown, and those work out well for many commuters. But it's tough to live in The Woodlands and bus/walk to Pearland. By the time you got to the office, they would've already replaced you with a combination of interns and robots.

This is all a big letdown moving here from somewhere such as Tokyo, London, or NYC. Not only is it difficult to walk or bike along major roads, it's also dangerous. People do it, and each to their own. But just know what you're getting into. And the heat means that walking even three blocks in a suit will leave you showing up to work smelling like a teenage opossum at least nine months out of the year.

I see I-10, but where is the Katy Freeway?

Houston freeways have nicknames

Many people don't use the technical names of the freeways around here. They use nicknames. And knowing these names comes in handy:

- **The Loop**

  When people say the Loop, they're referring to Loop 610, a 42-mile loop around the traditional center of the city.

- **All of the Loops (Yeah, the same Loop)**

  Depending where you are on the Loop, you're either on the North Loop, East Loop, South Loop, or West Loop.

- **The Beltway**

  This refers to Texas State Highway Beltway 8, or the Sam Houston Tollway, which forms an 88-mile circuit around the outer part of town.

- **The Grand Parkway**

  This is a reference to state Highway 99, the outermost and not-yet-complete tollway that loops around town, potentially linking a number of Houston suburbs together.

Nicknames Based on Destination

- Interstate 10 West, toward Katy from downtown, is known as the Katy Freeway. With 26 lanes across in certain parts, it's the largest freeway in Texas.

 **GETTING AROUND**

- Interstate 10 East, the same road toward Beaumont from downtown, is known as the Baytown East Freeway.
- Interstate 45 South, toward the Gulf of Mexico, is known as the Gulf Freeway. You can follow it straight to the seawall in Galveston.
- Interstate 45 North, the same road going from downtown toward Dallas, is known as the North Freeway.

Interstate 45 North is often called the North Freeway.

- Interstate 69/US Highway 59 going northeast towards Lufkin, Nacogdoches, and the rest of red dirt country, is known as the Eastex Freeway.
- Interstate 69/US Highway 59, same road from downtown going out toward Sugar Land, is called the Southwest Freeway, also known as the "Southworst."
- Highway 225, which runs out to all the plants around the Houston Ship Channel, is known as the La Porte Freeway. Smells like money.

Fact BOX

Did you know one of the big motivations behind the interstate system was the desire that citizens be able to move around quickly and easily in the event of a nuclear attack?

What's the RODEO like?

The Rodeo is a really big deal

Dating back to 1932, the Houston Livestock Show and Rodeo (HLSR) is one of the biggest parties in town. With events and festivities that span almost all of March, it's the largest rodeo in Texas, with bull riding, bareback riding, barrel racing, saddle bronc, steer wrestling, and tie-down and team roping. But that's just the beginning.

At the end of February, the World's Championship Bar-B-Que Contest pits elite barbecue teams against each other. Then the actual rodeo begins, as well as livestock competitions for beef cattle, dairy cattle, goats, rabbits, llamas, and other animals. There's also a big horse show and a number of animal competitions for kids, as well as big deal livestock auctions and sales. The whole thing has a fair-like atmosphere, with

Fact BOX

Practically every noteworthy country musician from Willie and Waylon to Charley Pride—and plenty of noncountry legends including Selena, Beyoncé, and Elvis—have played in the HLSR. You can see a complete list at https://www.rodeohouston.com/About-Us/History/Past-Entertainers.

NOT OUR FIRST RODEO

everything-on-a-stick type foods, rides for the kids, exhibitions of the latest pickup trucks, and more.

There's also a concert every single night until the rodeo is through. We're talking top billings in many different musical genres—many held at the ginormous NRG Stadium. There's even a wine garden where you can chill before shows. And it just goes on like this throughout March: rodeo and livestock and food and fun all day long, with nightly concerts.

Here are a few numbers from the 2019 HLSR to help you appreciate the scale: Total attendance for all activities that year reached more than 2.5 million. More than 34,000 volunteers helped make it all work. Prizes in excess of $2.1 million were awarded to rodeo contestants. Millions of dollars were raised for youth charities. And the closing concert with Lyle Lovett, Robert Earl Keen, and George Strait drew more than 80,000 people. I was there, and it was insane.

Tragically, the 2020 Houston Livestock Show and Rodeo was not canceled in time to prevent a performance by NCT 127.

Entrance of the 2020 HLSR during Go Tejano Day

Honey, have you seen my Luccheses?

In the movies or TV, when someone portrays Houston, they often show people moseying around downtown in boots, Wranglers, and black felt cowboy hats (in the summer). Some people do dress like that here; it's not weird. But Houstonians don't typically dress in Western wear every day. You have to go a little further south or west for that.

Houston doesn't have a cattle heritage like Fort Worth, San Antonio, or Abilene. Since the city's founding, we've been about cotton, oil, shipping, and so on. We've been far more likely to wear hard hats or neckties than Stetsons on the job. And today, though we may see just a skosh more boots than elsewhere in the country, we pretty much dress like any other warm-weather metropolis in America.

The exception? Go Texan Day.

Go Texan Day is widely acknowledged around town as the unofficial kickoff for the Houston Livestock Show and Rodeo. People all over from office buildings to schools dress up as if they were an extra on *Giant*: boots, buckles, hats—the lot. Sure, some people don't play along; the same bunch that never dresses up during Halloween. But a lot of people participate, and it's been a tradition for years. There's even an official citywide contest whereby your group can be recognized as the "most Texan."

Of course, this is still Texas. There are Houstonians who

 NOT OUR FIRST RODEO

dress like that every day, and they usually roll their eyes and chuckle at the urban accountants, surgeons, waitresses, and house spouses who suddenly look like they're about to go vaccinate a herd of dusty longhorns just the other side of the tank. But it's a bit of good-natured fun and an excuse to buy something to wear to the Rodeo in the coming weeks.

The Cavender's Boot City across from NRG Stadium does CRAZY business when Rodeo season rolls around.

Fact BOX

Where can you get rodeo gear? Everyday places include Boot Barn, Cavender's, Tecovas, and Gomez Western wear; Pinto Ranch is a rodeo favorite. For fancy custom boots, hit up Maida's, Republic, Parker, Tejas, Candela, Al's, and more.

Who are the Trail Riders?

Ushering in the rodeo with horsepower

Each year, thousands of people saddle up from all over Texas and Louisiana—many complete with covered wagons—to head to the Houston Livestock Show and Rodeo (HLSR). These "Trail Riders" are a tradition dating back to the 1950s, and spotting them along Texas highways is a statewide reminder that it's rodeo time in Houston.

There are 12 different "rides" that start from various Texas destinations and wind up in Houston for a big parade just prior to the rodeo. The Trail Riders meet at Memorial Park, transforming

The Sam Houston Trailriders are a group of around 100 riders in 17 wagons. They start in Montgomery and travel 75 miles into town.

it from just a bunch of joggers and golfers to a scene from a Zane Grey novel. Well, maybe it's more like a Zane Grey novel with accompanying motor homes, barbecue smokers, and port-a-cans. The Trail Riders then participate in a big parade that goes through downtown. It's the world's largest organized trail ride.

Each of the trail rides have different names, such as the "Salt Grass" and the "Old Spanish Trail." Within each, a number of wagons will participate. A "Trail Boss" keeps everything organized and safe along the way. Some of the wagons are sponsored by corporations such as H-E-B and Southwest Airlines. Others represent just families, friends, ranches, and neighbors looking for a fun ride.

The idea began on a bet made in the old Shamrock Hotel's Cork Room. Reese Lockett, mayor of Brenham at the time, was at a table complaining about a weather delay he'd experienced in Florida, proclaiming he'd never again travel so far away that he couldn't ride his horse back. Someone at the table expressed doubts the man could even ride from Brenham to Houston on horseback—and the bet was on. Reese made the ride, complete with a *Houston Chronicle* reporter to document the event. And it's been a rodeo tradition ever since.

Where are the *most exclusive* tents in town?

The World's Championship Bar-B-Que Contest

Many cities have exclusive events at which attendance makes one feel special. NYC has the $25,000 per plate Met Gala. Washington, DC, has the White House Correspondents' Dinner. And, yeah, we have black tie events for miles in this town—but one of Houston's most exclusive parties is the Houston Livestock Show and Rodeo (HLSR) World's Championship Bar-B-Que Contest—specifically, the team tents.

Officially kicking off the HLSR, 250 or more elite barbecue teams compete in categories such as champion brisket, ribs, chicken, and Dutch oven desserts. And the best of the best walks away with the Grand Champion title. For attendees, $20 will get you into NRG stadium, where you can eat barbecue at the Chuckwagon tent, check out a concert at the Garden stage, and do fun carnival stuff like ride rides and play midway games. It's fun. But what you really want to do is land a wristband to one of the exclusive barbecue team tents.

There's also a children's competition in which kids between the ages of 8 and 14 see who can make the best steak based on appearance, tenderness, and taste.

 NOT OUR FIRST RODEO

Prior to cook-off, a huge tent city is erected on a section of the NRG Stadium property with a tent for each competing team. And it really is a city—complete with electricity, little street signs, and everything. Inside each tent will be a big party in which a different team will serve up some of their delicious brisket, ribs, and whatever else is on the menu. Cold beer is available, live bands play, and many even have a dance floor. A lot of them look like little country bars, complete with neon signs.

You can buy tickets to the cook-off in general. But each of these hundreds of tents is private. You can't buy your way in; someone affiliated with the team has to give you a wristband. So start networking sometime around October for those wristbands, or you'll be left out in the cold like a plate of leftover potato salad.

Operation BBQ Relief celebrates a win earlier this year, but the real winners are the people they help every day. Learn more at operationbbqrelief.org. Photo courtesy of Operation BBQ Relief.

Fried Snickers? Cheesecake? Pecan pie?

The Fries of Texas are Upon You

Your cardiologist in the room? No? Sweet, let's talk about fried Oreos and stuff. Because while you're at the Houston Livestock Show and Rodeo (HLSR), you'll want to check out all the vendors selling old-school carnival foods such as funnel cakes, corn dogs, and anything-you-can-imagine on a stick. These specialty vendors come from all over the country to share both classic carnival treats and innovative new takes on fairway fare with rodeo visitors.

While I was there this year, I saw fried EVERYTHING—including Twinkies, Snickers bars, ice cream, key lime pie, s'mores, pickles, and pecan pie, as well as, of course, plenty of fried fruit pies. They were also selling donuts, mini-donuts, pretzels, churros, ice cream, funnel cakes, cinnamon rolls, roasted nuts, roasted corn, cheesecake, pizza, sausage, rattlesnake, kettle corn, tater tots, mac & cheese, root beer floats, burritos, and, naturally, barbecue.

Do you follow a vegan lifestyle and wonder what to eat at the Houston rodeo? Well, you're in luck, my friend, because Austin is just a short, three-hour drive west on HWY 290. Just go. Really. You'll be happier, and it will mean more for the rest of us.

The only problem is that unless you're a 13-year-old boy, there's only so much gluttony you can take in one sitting. So it's best to

 NOT OUR FIRST RODEO

bring a group so you can share orders of things; that way everybody gets a taste and can still fit onto the shuttle bus at the end of the evening.

There's even a behind-the-scenes contest. The rodeo assembles a panel of celebrity judges each year and declares select

Fried pecan pie? Fried cheesecake? No wonder Fried What! has won more than one Golden Buckle Foodie Award over the years.

carnival foods the best of the best with the Golden Buckle Foodie Awards. Here are just a few of the winners from the 2020 HLSR:

- Holmes Smokehouse's loaded waffle fries with shredded pork or beef
- Get Fried's donut chicken sandwich
- Burton Sausage's rib eye steak sandwich
- The Original Minneapple Pie's deep-fried cookie dough sundae
- Granny's Cheesecake & More's deep-fried cheesecake

Fact Box

The fried Oreo was invented by "Chicken Charlie" Boghosian, who works the San Diego County Fair and OC Fair. He's famous for deep-fried inventions that include the Krispy Kreme Chicken Ice Cream Sandwich, bacon-wrapped pickles, fried Kool-Aid and more.

Have you read the
WRITING
ON THE WALL?

You don't have to go to a museum to see some amazing works of art in H-Town. Sometimes you just have to walk down the street because there are hundreds of outdoor street art installations all around town. These range from high-profile commissioned murals on highly visible buildings to small, subtle pieces that may or may not have been exactly legal to create.

Sure, like any big city, we've got our share of plain old graffiti, but Houston boasts approximately 90 outdoor wall murals. Some of the most popular include the giant interpretation of Michelangelo's *The Creation of Man* with an aerosol spray can at 2800 San Jacinto, the Houston is Inspired mural at Preston and Travis Streets, the Montrose Paint Wall, and pretty much any building in EaDo (East of Downtown), the whole of which is tatted up like a Yakuza member. Follow @postwarbrit for some awesome EaDo street art.

Renowned more for its technical difficulty than aesthetics is the Be Someone mural over Interstate 45 going into downtown. Though not

 DEEP IN THE ART OF TEXAS

everyone is a fan, this illegally painted Union Pacific rail bridge has become a Houston icon. Every once in a while, someone will paint another message over it, and then it will be repaired—either by the original artist, whose identity remains secret, or by someone just wanting to bring back the inspirational message. As of this writing it reads: "Wash Ur Hands."

Houston was almost home to the nation's first graffiti museum—the Graffiti and Street Art Museum of Texas (though Hurricane Harvey suspended the opening and exhibitions). We did host the Houston Urban Experience Biennial Mural Art Festival, which drew dozens of artists from around the world last year. You could kill a whole day driving around looking at this stuff.

When you can paint like a Boss, you hit the Houston Graffiti Building at 1503 Chartres Street.

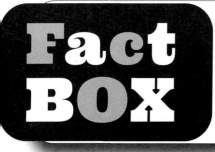

Fact BOX

So who creates all of this art? Dozens of artists, both anonymous and public, are the creators, including widely recognized names such as Sebastien Boileau, Mario E. Figueroa Jr., and Daniel Anguilu.

You drive a big, red shoe?

In most cities, a giant metal cockroach, complete with huge antennas, pulling up next to you at a red light would be worthy of note. But in Houston? It just means that it's time for the Houston Art Car Parade. The first and largest parade of its kind, Art Car lasts for days and culminates in a rolling showcase of 250 or more custom cars-turned-into-masterpieces. Contestants bring creations from 23 states, as well as Mexico and Canada.

The thing about driving a popcorn machine is that it's so easy to pop the clutch.

Over the years, I've seen an exact reproduction of the Family Truckster from National Lampoon's *Vacation*, boats made into cars, giant high-heeled shoes, rolling dragons, cars made of wood, multiple moving dinosaurs, hippie VWs, a Tiki bar on wheels, spaceships, a tribute to Stevie Ray Vaughn, giant skulls, a car with thousands of buttons stuck to it, a boxing robot, a pedal-operated fish, drivable toilets, and so much more.

Thousands of Houstonians set out lawn chairs, grab a cold drink, and enjoy these amazing rides roadside. The parade is held in April, when the weather is nice. It's officiated by a grand marshal, a role previously played by Dan Akroyd, Cheech Marin, football players J. J. Watt and Connor Barwin, Funkmaster George Clinton, and other notables such as politicians and astronauts.

 DEEP IN THE ART OF TEXAS

Fact BOX

Most people know the parade, but the event also includes a Main Street drag, a "Sneak Preview" at Discovery Green, a ball, and an awards ceremony.

Art Car has its roots in an arts organization called the Orange Show Foundation. In 1984, the Detering family donated a 1967 Ford station wagon to the Orange Show for auction at a gala. Artist Jackie Harris transformed the car into the "Fruitmobile" using $800 worth of paint and plastic fruit. She and other artists around town began creating cars for various festivals. They were wildly popular, so in 1988, the Orange Show organized the first ever Houston Art Car Parade, and the rest was history.

This may be a minivan, but there's a major smackdown about to happen.

So artists PAINT the signal boxes?

In appreciation of practical masterpieces

Though people rarely notice them, each stoplight around town has a signal box full of electronics that controls the lights and makes the mechanics of it all work. While they keep everyone alive, they're not much to look at—except in Houston—where they are actually quite something to see thanks to a number of Texas artists.

Professional artists with a variety of different styles have turned these functional traffic signal boxes into beautiful works of art citywide. The next time you're stopped at a light, look around for one. More than 220 have been completed—including paintings of hummingbirds, Martin Luther King Jr., bald eagles, deer in the sunset, jellyfish, seagulls, bicycles, abstract designs, butterflies, cityscapes, bookshelves, Frida Kahlo, Dr. Red Duke, and more.

The Up Art Studio, which specializes in public art projects, worked with the City of Houston to put the first of these "Mini

Fact BOX

About Houston stoplights: When the light turns green, don't just step on the gas. Look both ways first. People run lights in this town like crazy, and the habit could save your life.

 DEEP IN THE ART OF TEXAS

Murals" into place in 2015. The project was intended to bring art to the public, as well as to deter graffiti. The thinking is that someone is less likely to spray paint something like "Flapjack was here" on a traffic control box if there's already a beautiful work of art on the box. Does it work? Pretty much. And the resulting initiative has brought something interesting and fresh to a number of Houston neighborhoods.

More than a dozen talented artists have participated in this effort, some painting under their real names and others operating under a *nome d'arte*. Nonprofits, grants, businesses, Houston City Council offices, and other donors pay for the initiative. Up Art Studio also creates Mini Murals in Austin. You can visit minimurals.org to see these painted traffic boxes in Houston and Austin, complete with a detailed map. You can also follow #MiniMurals on Twitter and Instagram.

This box at the Houston Zoo features a different creature on each side . . . and you don't have to clean up after any of them.

This Mini Mural was painted by Wiley Houston and stands at Center Street and Heights Boulevard.

Who's got the BEST seats in the South?

Houston's Theater District

Another thing that shocks so many who are new to the Houston area is H-Town's world-class theater district. The Houston Theater District has the highest concentration of theater seats in a downtown area anywhere outside of New York City. It's composed of several heavyweight performing arts venues and companies, including the Alley Theatre, Jones Hall, Wortham Theater Center, and the Hobby Center for the Performing Arts.

Spanning 17 blocks downtown, it hosts not just multiple theater and performance stages but also the Houston Ballet, the Houston Grand Opera, the Houston Symphony, and a number of other world-class companies. And, with a number of restaurants and bars nearby, you can make dinner and a show without fighting rush-hour traffic.

The Alley is the Theater District's centerpiece. A Houston institution, the Alley is actually one of the nation's largest nonprofit theaters. It produces 16 plays per year under the artistic direction of Rob Melrose, who has an MFA in Directing from the Yale School of Drama and has done just about everything in the world of theater. And then there's Jones Hall, which more than 400,000 Houstonians visit each year to hear Houston's world-class symphony. Our symphony is one of the oldest arts organizations in Texas, with an operating budget of more than $35M and 88 full-time professional musicians.

 DEEP IN THE ART OF TEXAS

Wortham Theater Center is home to both the Houston Ballet and the Houston Grand Opera. The Houston Ballet has a staff of 59 and has toured nationally and internationally. Its production of the Nutcracker has become a family tradition for decades (as has the accompanying Nutcracker Market at NRG Stadium). The Houston Grand Opera is one of the largest and most acclaimed opera companies in the nation—touring extensively and taking home Tonys, Emmys, and Grammys.

And scene

Built in 1966, Jones Hall is home to the Houston Symphony.

Why is it called the Alley Theatre? Well, when it first started, the whole thing ran on a shoestring, and performances were actually held in an affordable space literally in an alley off Main Street.

What's up with the RAP SCENE?

Houston hits hard

Rap as a genre may have begun in 1970s NYC, but Houston would soon make its mark—dealing with the same socioeconomic issues as African American communities on the East Coast and in Los Angeles, hungry for a voice, and determined to put in the work despite the lack of early respect by the mainstream industry.

Respect for H-Town rappers on the East side (The Screwed Up Click)

The Geto Boys were the first local group to break out nationally. A product of J. Prince's powerhouse Rap-a-Lot record label, their hit "My Mind is Playing Tricks on Me" gave depth to the genre, blew up around the world, and put H-Town on the map for hard-core Southern rap. These guys put the hardscrabble lifestyle of the streets out there, 100 percent raw and unfiltered. One album cover features a real-life picture of Bushwick Bill (RIP) being rolled on a hospital gurney after shooting himself in the face high on PCP and drunk on Everclear. Dude.

Around 1990, Robert Earl Davis Jr., who performed under the name DJ Screw, put his own spin on the scene. A DJ rather than a rapper, Davis slowed things down with a sluggish, haunting tempo and precision cuts. This new "chopped and screwed" style was first heard only around here but eventually caught on around the world. It also coincided with the rise of "lean," a mixture of codeine and Sprite (and sometimes hard candy) that for many paired with DJ Screw's music like Hendrix and LSD. A relentless workaholic, DJ Screw passed away of a heart attack in 2000.

Other Houston rappers to make it big since have included acts such as Pimp C, Paul Wall, Travis Scott, Slim Thug, Lil' Flip, Bun B, Devin the Dude, Chamillionaire, Z-Ro, Fat Pat, Lil' Keke, Street Military, Big HAWK, Trae Tha Truth, Baby Bash, Mike Jones, and many more.

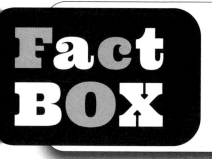

Fact BOX

Want a deep dive into H-Town's rap roots, compete with *vérité*-style photography by Peter Beste? Check out *Houston Rap Tapes* by Lance Scott Walker (University of Texas Press).

SAM HOUSTON (page 162)

THE RAP SCENE (page 82)

DR. RED DUKE (page 166)

THE WRITING ON THE WALL (page 74)

TACO TUESDAY (page 38)

WILD PEACOCKS (page 112)

QUINCEAÑERA (page 16)
Photo courtesy of Anelale Nájera via Unsplash

RAMP UP YOUR CULTURE AND YOUR STEP COUNT (page 128)

BLUEBONNET MADNESS (page 106)

HOUSTON THEATER DISTRICT (page 80)

THE NUTCRACKER MARKET (page 132)

WHAT THE #&*! IS A WARD? (page 34)

ASTRODOME (page 158)

What's better than a *lifetime* collecting art?

It's not unusual for couples to pursue hobbies together when they get married. For example, my wife married a writer, so our new hobbies included showing up places uninvited for free drinks and making up ever-more-incredulous lies for creditors. But when John de Menil and Dominique Schlumberger married in Paris, John began opening his wife's eyes to the wonder of the arts. And it was a lifelong journey from which all of Houston would eventually benefit.

The couple began collecting art seriously in the mid-1940s and became patrons for the next several decades both at home and abroad. Eventually, they brought together what some have called one of the finest personal art collections of the modern era—a collection that's grown to more than 17,000 works today. A number of influences helped shape the collection over the years,

Fact BOX

The Rothko Chapel has inspired millions. But for all his acclaim, Rothko never got to see his Houston chapel in action; he committed suicide shortly before it opened.

 DEEP IN THE ART OF TEXAS

including the couple's personal passion not only for modern art and progressive ideas but also for world travel, French culture, the Catholic church, a number of social causes, and the desire to share the power of art with the public.

John de Menil passed away in 1973. In the 1980s, Dominique de Menil decided to turn her family's private collection into a museum in a building designed by architect Renzo Piano. The Menil Collection includes modern and contemporary art, surrealism, and medieval and Byzantine art, along with arts of the Pacific Islands, the Ancient World, Africa, the Americas, and the Pacific Northwest. There's also an amazing drawings collection and more. Today, the facility encompasses several buildings, a park, a drawing institute, a bookstore, and a bistro. The campus also includes the Rothko Chapel—a collection of 14 commissioned works by abstract expressionist Mark Rothko housed in a Philip Johnson-designed building that inspires spiritual reflection and interfaith dialogue.

The Menil Collection has an extensive collection of Byzantine art. The Byzantine Empire existed from 330 to 1453. Photo courtesy of the Menil Collection.

What is a bayou, anyway?

Houston has had a number of nicknames since its founding, but "the Bayou City" is the one that's stuck for the most part. Just what is a bayou, anyway? Is it a river? A swamp? Some combination of the two?

A bayou is just a slow-moving creek, or an especially swampy section of a lake or river. People often associate bayous with Louisiana. And, in fact, we take the word bayou from a French creole adaptation of the Choctaw word bayuk, which meant "small stream." Though many today know the Choctaw Native American peoples as Oklahoma residents, they are actually indigenous to Mississippi, Alabama, and parts of Louisiana. So they knew a bayou when they saw one.

Houston actually has 22 distinct bayous and waterways scattered around town. Buffalo Bayou is the largest and longest of them, a sort of 53-mile squiggly signature that runs from Katy to downtown. Buffalo Bayou's waters flow into the Houston Ship Channel, then Galveston Bay and then the Gulf of Mexico. During storm seasons, there is also a small chance that Buffalo Bayou may take a slight detour to your home along the way out of town, where it may attempt to move in with you and your family.

Despite the complex issues with flooding Houston has had over the years, most Houstonians grow to love the bayous' muddy waters. Tons of wildlife live in and around them, and they help

 NATURAL SURROUNDINGS

create dozens of bayou-side wilderness areas and parks. Buffalo Bayou Park alone is 160 acres of lush green space with a number of trails and attractions. Improvements to bayou-side park spaces have been nonstop for decades. One recent example is the Bayou Greenways project, which connects 3,000 acres of green space via 150 miles of bike trail running alongside many of Houston's bayous. See you on the trails!

Buffalo Bayou at Buffalo Bayou Park.

Some bayous are actually driven not just by physical topography but also by tidal forces, so that when the moon is just right, they can actually flow backward and slightly uphill.

Why is that family posing in the flowers?

Bluebonnets (*Lupinus texensis*) are native Texan flowers that bloom annually somewhere around mid-March to early April. During the six weeks or so they're in bloom, they put people all across Texas in a good mood. The official state flower since 1901, their vibrant blue color and pleasant scent are like a peace offering before the heat starts beating you down like a cage fighter high on PCP.

Houstonians go nuts taking pictures during bluebonnet season. Families put their kids among the blooms to pose. Dog owners place their pampered pooches in fields for pictures. Singles kick back in bluebonnets for Texas-style profile pics. Some even hire a professional photographer. In some of the most popular spots around town, you might even

Families take pics all around town during bluebonnet season, like these guys at Terry Hershey Park.

have to wait until others are done with the best patches before posing.

Here are a few of the best spots to see bluebonnets around town:

- Along Buffalo Bayou, in Terry Hershey Park, and downtown in places such as Spots Park
- Memorial Park, potentially distracting you from the pain of running
- Along White Oak Bayou north of Interstate 10
- Blessington Farms in Wallis just west of Houston
- Along Interstate 10 just west of Katy

It's also nice to take a drive through the country during bluebonnet season, as they grow statewide. Some regional wineries even participate in the Texas Bluebonnet Wine Trail, whereby you can drive from winery to winery and enjoy the wildflowers in bloom along the way.

Bluebonnets only grow in three US. states—Texas, Louisiana, and Florida. They're actually members of the legume family. Growing up, I was always told that it was illegal to pick them, but that's just a local myth. It is considered rude to pick them or crush them, though, so do that sort of thing at your own risk.

"The bluebonnet is to Texas what the shamrock is to Ireland, the cherry blossom to Japan, the lily to France, the rose to England, and the tulip to Holland." —Historian Jack Maguire

Fact BOX

What are those black birds in the parking lot?

Grackles, grackles everywhere

Sometimes in Houston, especially around dusk, you'll see hundreds—maybe even thousands—of black birds all perched on cars, power lines, light poles, street signs, and other high-up places. These are the same birds you see hopping around in the H-E-B parking lot looking for a stray French fry or bathing in rainwater on the sidewalk. They're grackles, and they pretty much do whatever the #&!@ they want in this town.

The great tailed grackle (*Quiscalus mexicanus*) can be found all over Texas and the Southwest—as well as Mexico and Central America. Male grackles are big and black, with a bluish-purple sheen and bright yellow eyes; females are smaller and a dullish brown. They're part of the Icteridae family, the same species of songbird as orioles and blackbirds. Their song is an acquired taste, however, creating a variety of sounds that seem more likely to originate from an auto mechanic than a bird's beak.

Still, they're a part of life in Houston as they've thrived in urban environments over the centuries. At night, they prefer sleeping in large groups so that they can warn each other or get away if a predator such as a hawk or owl tries to make one a meal. And with its scattered trees, varied perching areas, and access to food and water, the Houston cityscape is the perfect environment.

 NATURAL SURROUNDINGS

A lot of people think they're a nuisance. I complain about them in jest, but they're amazingly adaptable. When I cut my grass, a large male grackle follows behind me and eats the bugs just made available by the freshly shorn blades. They've grown on me, and many who live in the city appreciate their tenacity. That said, it doesn't hurt to get your car waxed every few months for when you inevitably park underneath them.

Male grackles are darker and more iridescent. Females are brownish with a subtle stripe above their eye; this male also apparently smokes menthols.

Fact BOX

In winter, grackles roost together in huge numbers. The Rio Grande Valley sugar cane fields can have up to 500,000 birds in a group! That's a lot of grackle.

Where can I learn about nature in the city?

The Houston Arboretum & Nature Center

These days, it's easy for city dwellers to feel disconnected from the natural world. But it's good to know at least a little about the trees, plants, and animals all around you. In Houston, the place to start is with a trip to the Houston Arboretum & Nature Center. The 155-acre Arboretum is on the western edge of Memorial Park, just inside the West Loop. The experience basically has three parts: a visitor's center, nature trails, and special events.

The indoor exhibition showcases local plants, trees, and animals, and it's totally free except for parking. Visitors can see all kinds of museum-quality displays showcasing different types of native Southeast Texas flora and fauna. It's not a huge place like the Houston Museum of Natural Science, but it's well thought-out, beautiful, and super educational. In fact, as of this writing, the facility itself is undergoing a big renovation that will make it better than ever. But the actual building is only part of the experience.

Fact BOX

Squirrels are big, fat liars! Squirrels are scatter hoarders, burying acorns and stuff all around to eat later. But they also pretend to bury food with absolutely nothing in their little paws in order to throw off squirrely thieves.

NATURAL SURROUNDINGS

The Arboretum also has outdoor nature trails where you can see many of these species in real life, complete with little informative placards. There are 13 different trails, none too long or physically challenging for most. And together, they let you explore a variety of different wildlife habitats native to the Houston area, including prairies, savannahs, ravines, wetlands, and woodlands.

And then there are all the cool classes, tours, scavenger hunts, bird surveys, lectures, and more. These range from romantic dinners on the trails complete with wine to fun activities for kids all year around. There are even free guided tours! So disconnect that smartphone and reconnect with nature before you end up smoking poison oak or trying to pick up a water moccasin or something.

The Arboretum's programs for grown-ups include gardening classes, the "Arboretum at Night" bat walks, night hikes, wine and cheese tastings, art and photo lessons, and more.

Wait, Houston has WILD peacocks?

Yep, peacocks around the block

Wild peafowl (that's peacocks and peahens) run loose in some neighborhoods, mostly on the westside but also reportedly in other parts of town such as Uptown or near William P. Hobby Airport. Each day when my wife runs a certain route, she's inevitably followed by a long-legged peacock that runs alongside her for a half-block or so before ruffling his plumage and going off to find a more suitable, and catchable, mate. Can't blame a guy for trying.

In most cases, nobody really owns these birds; different people feed them, and they just sort of run around doing their peafowl thing. Some residents love them; giving them names, feeding them, and visiting with them every day. Others consider them a nuisance and discourage the fostering of neighborhood populations. We think they're super cool, but we only see them in our 'hood occasionally.

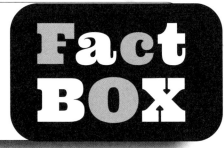

Peahens have love antennae! The crest on top of a peahen's head has little built-in sensors on top that detect the motion of a peacock shaking his tail feathers far away.

Fact BOX

NATURAL SURROUNDINGS

These birds are not indigenous to Texas. The specific type you see running around here are actually Indian peafowl (*Pavo cristatus*), and native to the subcontinent. Their most common origin story here in town is that a couple who lived on White Wing Lane across the bayou from Lakeside Country Club introduced them. Apparently, a husband bought his wife a pair back in 1980. Today there are hundreds.

Despite massive tail feathers, peafowl can fly—just not very far. During Harvey, bevies of peafowl around our neighborhood sought refuge on top of houses to escape the floodwaters (as did many of us). But the peafowl population made it through relatively unscathed. Their unmistakable call makes most people involuntarily recoil and close one eye; they sound like two feral cats in a knife fight. Still, they're an interesting sight that make some people look twice and have made Houston their home.

Despite their big ol' trains, peacocks can actually fly.

MAN VS. MOSQUITO:
Who's winning?

Our victory is not certain

If you're going to live in Houston, you'll need to protect yourself against mosquitoes. More than 50 species of mosquitoes can be found here, and some nights it feels like all of them are trying to eat you like a school of piranha. Among the most common are the Asian tiger mosquito (*Aedes albopictus*), marsh mosquitoes (*Anopheles quadrimaculatus*), and the common house mosquito (*Culex pipiens*).

According to one recent study, Houston isn't the worst US city when it comes to these buzzy pests; that honor went to Atlanta. But Houston did rank No. 5, just behind Chicago. Washington, D.C., ranked just third in terms of blood-sucking parasites, but they'll always be No. 1 in my book. Mosquitoes become a problem when the weather gets warm—peaking in August and September. Most hide during the day, coming out to feed at dawn and dusk.

Mosquito bites aren't just annoying; they can transmit serious diseases such as malaria, West Nile, yellow fever, Zika virus, dengue fever, St. Louis encephalitis, and cooties. So get your guard up. Here's how:

- Pour out any standing water around the house.
- Wear long sleeves if practical.
- Consider patio ceiling fans; mosquitoes hate moving air.

 NATURAL SURROUNDINGS

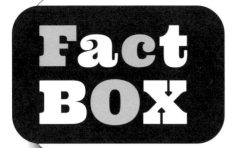

- Apply EPA–approved mosquito repellent (first sunscreen, then bug spray).
- Ask your spouse to go out first, serving as a distraction.

In summer evenings, it's not unusual to see trucks deployed around town spraying huge plumes of insecticide from street to street as a public service.

Are you one of those people who gets bit way more than others? It's a thing. Turns out mosquitoes find you especially yummy if you have Type O blood, are pregnant, have been drinking beer, carry a higher body temperature, are wearing a color that makes you easy to find, or have been working out.

Only female mosquitoes bite; males get their nutrients from plants. Photo courtesy of Syed Ali via Unsplash.

WHAT just *flew* by me?

Houston is pretty much one giant bat habitat

We live next door to Club Westside (formerly known as the Westside Tennis Club). In the evenings, huge banks of lights are switched on to allow for nighttime tennis. If you study these lights closely, you'll notice moths and other bugs are drawn to them. And every once in a while, something dark and barely visible in the night sky snatches one of the bugs from the air. It's a bat—one of Houston's best allies in the War on Bugs.

Texas has the largest diversity of bats in the nation, with more than 30 species found scattered around the state. You'll find 11 different species here in Houston, including the most common, *Tadarida brasiliensis*, otherwise known as the Brazilian or Mexican free-tailed bat. While they typically live in caves, they've made themselves at home in Houston over the decades—roosting under bridges, beneath the overhangs of buildings or houses, and basically wherever they feel comfortable.

And why do some Houstonians love to see them come around? Because they eat mosquitoes—lots and lots of mosquitoes. A single bat can eat up to 1,200 in an hour and up to 8,000 bugs nightly—all without dangerous chemicals or throwing off the local ecosystem. They're like nature's little bug zappers—a tiny warm-blooded cleaning crew that sleeps quietly during the day and works in the evening. While some people call pest control

NATURAL SURROUNDINGS

professionals to get rid of them, others put up bat houses to help attract them.

Houston's most famous bat colony is the one beneath the Waugh Drive Bridge between Memorial Drive and Allen Parkway. Though hard hit by Harvey, this colony is still going strong with thousands of little fuzzy members. Each night people gather around to catch a glimpse of them feeding.

There's an observation area near the Waugh Street Bridge filled with fun facts. Trivia: the oldest living bat is 41 years old.

Fact BOX

Many fear bats because of a perception they carry rabies. But rabid bats are actually extremely rare. Don't handle them or bother them, and you'll be fine.

What's the deal with high school football?

Texas is known for having the best high school football teams in the nation, and even within that elite environment, Houston-area teams stand strong. According to MaxPreps in 2019, the state's first ranked team was North Shore (15-1). Katy came in at No. 4 with a record of 12-1, and Pearland's Shadow Creek hit at No. 6 with a record of 16-0. Keep in mind that all these elite championship schools are within a 30-minute drive from each other.

Sure, parents watch their kids play like at any other high school nationwide, but so do alums and just people who love good football. These games are played on Friday nights, so football fans can watch high school games Friday, college games on Saturday, and the NFL on Sunday. Cowboys fans can even watch high-school-level play on Sunday too (kidding).

Texas is a major source for Division I university recruits, so you'll find recruiters in the stands from UT Austin, Texas A&M, Texas Tech, and other Lone Star schools as well as from all around the country. In fact, Texas schools have to fight to keep talent in state, lest we be forced to eventually line up against them on the other side of the line of scrimmage.

And then there are the stadiums. At $70.3 million, Katy's Mike Johnston Field at Legacy Stadium is widely reported as the most

 SPORTS AND OUTDOORS

expensive high school football stadium in Texas as of this writing. The video screen alone cost $1.8 million. Barry Field in Northwest Houston cost $80 million to build, including an arena and theater. Scheduled to open in 2020, the new Tomball ISD district stadium is set to cost $51.2 million. Woodforest State Bank Stadium in Conroe? $49 million. And Freedom Field in Alvin ISD cost a cool $41.4 million.

The popular show *Friday Night Lights* starring Kyle Chandler was inspired by H. G. Bissinger's book about the Permian Panthers. And where did the playoff teams wind up? Yep, Houston's Astrodome.

A Katy running back puts on the moves. Photo courtesy of Keith Johnston via Unsplash.

Is Galveston worth visiting?

The shore next door

If you take Interstate 45 South until it dead ends, you'll end up in the city of Galveston on Galveston Island. OK, so let's get this out of the way: the water right around Galveston is a sort of muddy brownish-greenish-yellow. It looks more like the Thames than Phuket, and the beaches sport the occasional naturally occurring tar ball. But for more than 150 years, Houstonians have had fun in Galveston soaking up sun on the beach, fishing, taking a stroll along the seawall, and more.

Galveston has a fascinating history full of Karankawa natives, explorers, pirates, the Republic of Texas Navy, tragic storms, gangsters, buried treasure, heroes, engineers, big business, ghost tales, and other interesting phenomenon. And today, it's a vibrant tourist destination and beloved Texas treasure whose awesomeness couldn't possibly be contained in a book like this. But here, in no particular order, are 20 quick reasons H-Town loves its sister by the sea.

Fact Box

1417 Harborside in Galveston holds the ruins of Jean Lafitte's former home, Maison Rouge—a site said to be haunted. For details, read *Ghosts of Galveston* by Kathleen Shanahan Maca.

 SPORTS AND OUTDOORS

1. The insane American Institute of Architects sandcastle competition
2. The 19th-century Victorian Dickens on the Strand Christmas celebration
3. The Lone Star Rally's rowdy fun with thousands of motorcycles
4. Charter fishing trips of both Galveston Bay and the Gulf of Mexico
5. Catching a cruise on Carnival, Royal Caribbean, or Disney
6. Taking a dolphin-watching tour on a dolphin-safe boat
7. Historic commercial and residential architecture
8. Texas's most popular Mardi Gras celebration
9. Checking out a real-life drilling rig at Pier 21
10. Hanging out on the Seawall
11. The 1877 Tall Ship *Elissa*
12. The Spot's five different themed bars
13. Antique shopping on The Strand Historic District
14. Galveston Fishing Pier
15. Brunch, and maybe ghosts, at the Hotel Galvez
16. Seafood at Gaidos Seafood Restaurant
17. Soaking up rays at Stewart Beach
18. Catching a 4D Special FX movie at Moody Gardens
19. Getting cultural at The Grand 1894 Opera House
20. Strolling around the Galveston Island Historic Pleasure Pier

Galveston Island has 32 miles of beach in total. Photo courtesy of Jon Ade Holder via Unsplash.

How strong is Houston's cycling community?

Houston is not known for being a bike-friendly community like Austin or Seattle. In fact, much like Los Angeles, it has a well deserved reputation for being a dangerous place to ride—even a deadly place. I've had more than one friend hit by a car while riding, and one that did not survive (RIP David Rosenfeld; we miss you, brother). And, yet, Houston has a surprisingly robust and active cycling community.

There are cycling groups of all levels who ride here, from hard-core training outfits to slow social rides more concerned with networking and a cold beer afterwards. Some have their origin with different bike shops around town, others simply started as a group of friends or neighbors. There are rides happening all day, every day, and each has its own unique flavor. Check out bikehouston.org to find your fit.

One of the most popular group rides is Critical Mass (CriticalMassHouston.com). This casual, welcoming ride happens every last Friday of the month. The group meets downtown at Guadalupe Park in the evening and rides between 18 and 25 miles at a slow to moderate pace. And you don't need a $20,000 Italian road bike made of unicorn dust that weighs half-a-gram;

 SPORTS AND OUTDOORS

A group of cyclists ride down Washington Avenue at the end of a workday.

Houston's infrastructure gets more bike-friendly every year, with millions of dollars in ongoing improvements underway. Visit HoustonBikePlan.org for the latest.

some people just rent B-Cycle bikes to join in. With thousands of participants, they basically take over the road—and the bars.

The BP MS150 Houston to Austin ride is Houston's most popular road race. Benefitting the National Multiple Sclerosis Society, more than 9,000 riders participate. Most major Houston corporations have sponsored MS 150 race teams, as well as just groups of friends who want to take on a tough challenge and do a little good along the way. Each participant is required to raise a minimum of $400 for the cause.

Where are all the soccer fans?

In most of Texas, when a boy tells his father that he wants to play soccer, the father will calmly encourage him, excuse himself, walk out to the driveway, and sob silently in his Chevy Silverado. The United States, and Texas in particular, is not known for being a soccer-loving land. But while this might still be true in a few Houston households, soccer fans generally find Houston a lot more accommodating than the rest of the state.

First, you'll meet fans here of whichever team you follow, from Colombia to Cameroon. We have 91 consulates, so fans from both the United States and around the world can find their people and cheer on their team. The British can even find fellow English Football Legue (EFL) fans (come on, you R's!) and follow their teams at places such as the Richmond Arms.

Next, we have our own Major League Soccer team, the Houston Dynamo. Also known as the Orange Crush, or La Naranja, they hold it down at BBVA Stadium. Fans tailgate before the games, the crowd is raucous but polite, the team is good, the beer is cold, and the stadium is nice on a mild night. And it all happens to the beat of El Batallón, a club band made up of supporters whose endurance and energy seems to rival the players on game day. We also have the Dynamo's sister team, the Houston Dash—our home team in the National Women's Soccer League.

 SPORTS AND OUTDOORS

Both the Dynamo and the Dash play at BBVA Stadium on the east side.

Like to play? There are tons of great places. Many parks have a soccer field, though you typically have to book them in advance, and there are multiple indoor and outdoor spaces ranging from free to fancy. There are also leagues for both kids and adults, and don't forget the Houston Toros Soccer Facility on Summer Street.

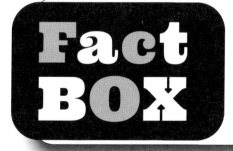

Each year, the Houston Dynamo and Dallas FC shoot it out for a series championship known as the Texas Derby, whereby the winner claims a cannon known as *El Capitán*.

Who's got more park space than any other Top 10 US city?

That's right, Houstonians like it green

When people from outside Texas envision Houston, they sometimes mistakenly think of dust and cowboys and whatnot. When people from elsewhere in Texas envision Houston, they think of a corporate hellscape of office buildings and refineries in which someone steals the wheels off your car 10 minutes after you park. Neither of these is accurate, however. They can get your wheels in about three minutes, and also your tailgate! Kidding. Sort of.

But the thing nobody sees coming is Houston's wonderful green space. This place is packed with wide-open parks where people jog, read, work out, practice tai chi, walk, and do whatever else people do when they're free-range humans. The City of Houston park system alone has approximately 38,394 acres of green space and that's not including nearby county and state parks or private land made available to the public.

According to The Trust for Public Land, the national average of park acres per thousand residents is 18.8, but Houston boasts around 27.2 park acres per thousand residents.

 SPORTS AND OUTDOORS

There are 366 parks and 200 additional green spaces within the Houston parks system.

Memorial Park off of Memorial Drive was named in homage to the land's service as a World War I training camp called Camp Logan. Almost 100 years old as of this writing, the park spans 1,464.21 acres and includes a three-mile loop running trail, golf course, tennis courts, nature trails, baseball field, fitness center, pool, random sports meet ups, Beck's Prime burger joint complete with patios, and more.

Buffalo Bayou Park spans 160 acres between Memorial Drive and Allen Parkway just west of downtown. In addition to being a big, beautiful green space in which you can do whatever you want, it has a skate park, an underground cistern, a dog park, a bat colony, jogging trails, and tons of activities from yoga to poetry.

And Terry Hershey Park on the westside stretches along Buffalo Bayou from the West Belt to Katy—offering on- and off-road trails, wildlife, wildflowers, all kinds of amenities, and people doing interesting things.

Into culture and your step count?

Houston has more than 150 museums scattered around town, ranging from epic affairs to the small, quirky, and private museums that can be so much fun. And the centerpiece of Houston's museum action is in the Houston Museum District: 18 museums within nine square miles that comprise one of the largest concentrations of cultural institutions in the nation. And, pro tip, each Thursday admission to many Houston Museum District venues is free simply as a public service.

Museum District highlights include:

Houston Museum of Natural Science
This 433,000-square-foot institution has extensive collections and exhibits on paleontology, African and Texas wildlife, astronomy, entomology, energy, indigenous cultures of the Americas, ancient Egypt, chemistry, gems and minerals, and malacology, along with tons of temporary exhibitions. Check out the Cockrell Butterfly Center and

Opened in 1909, the Houston Museum of Natural Science has five floors of permanent exhibits ranging from space to seashells.

 UNIQUE EVENTS AND DESTINATIONS

Weiss Energy Hall while you're there.

Museum of Fine Arts, Houston

The city's flagship fine arts museum, the Museum of Fine Arts, Houston, holds a staggering collection and offers a number of amazing temporary exhibitions that mean it's not a once-and-done experience. The museum is composed of two huge gallery buildings, a sculpture garden, two house museums (Rienzi and the Bayou Bend Collection and Gardens), more than one art school, a library, a movie theater, and a pretty lively happy hour on Thursdays.

The Houston Museum District has 19 museums spread across four different walking zones.

Children's Museum Houston

With more than 20 different exhibits, games, and activities, the Children's Museum is a must if you have kids, and it's also a fun place to throw a party. Exhibits include: Constructioneering, which lets kids don a hard hat and try their hand at design, engineering, and construction; the How Does it Work? exhibition, which lets you do hands-on investigation; and its Chevron Maker Annex, which lets kids play with 3D printers, laser cutters, and more.

Fact BOX

While you're in the area you can also hit up the Houston Zoo, Hermann Park (stop by the Japanese garden), Miller Outdoor Theater, Lucille's, and the bar at Hotel ZaZa.

Do real-life astronauts still live here?

Houston is still Space City

Aerospace has changed a lot over the years, from globalization to Elon Musk's SpaceX; and many these days seem to take space travel for granted. But Houston is still home to Johnson Space Center (JSC), its astronauts, and the legions of other scientists, pilots, engineers, and other experts it takes to make space travel work.

Houston has been inextricably linked with space flight since the late 1950s. JSC in the Houston suburb of Clear Lake still has a mission to "lead human space exploration." It supports International Space Station operations, a new craft called Orion, missions to the moon and Mars, biomedical research, and hundreds of other initiatives.

There are 48 active astronauts at NASA, and the odds of running into one around Clear Lake are not out of this world. Around 110 astronauts work at JSC, as does a civilian workforce of around 3,000 really impressive people. So there's more here than merely the setting for Larry McMurtry's *Terms of Endearment* novel. You don't even have to visit NASA to see its influence around town, with businesses such as Neil's Bahr (an allusion to Danish physicist Niels Bohr), Black Hole Coffee, Star Pizza, and True Anomaly Brewing—which is owned by a group of current and former NASA employees.

Houston has hosted astronauts as they have learned, trained, worked, and commanded from JSC. Back in the 1960s, the Timber

 UNIQUE EVENTS AND DESTINATIONS

There are lots of things to do at JSC, but none compare to the Level 9 tour—a four- or five-hour VIP experience taking you behind the scenes.

Grove neighborhood in Clear Lake was home to many prominent astronauts, including Gus Grissom, Scott Carpenter, and John Glenn. The neighborhood pool is shaped like the Mercury space capsule, and residents used to have "splashdown parties" to celebrate successful space missions. And with what the men and women at JSC are up to these days, there will be more space-themed celebrations to come around H-Town.

Replica of the space shuttle at Space Center Houston. Photo courtesy of Erick F. Castaneda via Unsplash.

What's the Nutcracker Market all about?

Ho-ho-ho, man, my feet are killing me

Each year the Houston Ballet puts on an enormous holiday-themed shopping experience at NRG Stadium called the Nutcracker Market. The purpose is ostensibly to raise money for the Houston Ballet Foundation, but its even more critical purpose is to make sure your home's holiday decorations out-festive, out-shine, out-spirit, and out-jolly your neighbors'—that and to give ladies an excuse to drink mimosas.

And husbands everywhere absolutely love it!

OK, that's not entirely true. Actually, most husbands huddle in groups at the Nutcracker Market dutifully escorting their wives, nodding at other guys in line at the beer stand and sneaking glances at ESPN Gamecast on their smartphones. "Honey, if you like that six-foot Rudolph with the cowboy hat and light-up nose, you should totally buy it," they say as they stare off into space.

But the Nutcracker Market is a Houston tradition to kick-start holiday decorating, get a jump on shopping, and support the ballet. The event started in 1981 as a church bazaar and has evolved over the years into a massive affair. People come from miles around to shop at the Nutcracker Market. Christmas tree lights and decorations? Check. Texas-themed holiday decor? Check. Yule-tide dog collars, socks, holiday fudge, candy canes, hats, clothes, toys,

 UNIQUE EVENTS AND DESTINATIONS

purses, and other gifts? You bet your jingle bells.

And the event does raise a ton of money. Last year, people dropped about $20M among the 250+ merchants selling at the event, plus the modest admission fee. All the admission bucks and 11 percent of the take from each stall goes to support the Houston Ballet. The Nutcracker Market is so popular that they actually started doing it twice a year: the traditional fall market and another in spring that's all Easter bunnies and flowers and such.

The Nutcracker Market is a tradition for many family and friends, with people coming from all around to attend. Photo by Fulton Davenport at PWL Studio, courtesy of the Nutcracker Market.

Fact BOX

Don't miss the actual production of *The Nutcracker*. Hey, you're going to hear the Dance of the Sugar Plum Fairy 600,000 times throughout the season; you might as well associate it with something beautiful.

Is the Miller Outdoor Theatre really free?

On many evenings when the weather is nice, if you stroll down to Hermann Park in the Museum District, between the Houston Museum of Natural Science and the Houston Zoo, you'll see an incredible sight: thousands will be gathered on the lush, green grass around a large, open-air theater. They'll be splayed out on blankets and draped over lawn chairs; some are sipping wine or cold drinks and eating picnic food; couples are laying down, arms around each other, and kids are rolling down the grassy hills like they're on a roller coaster. They'll all be watching a concert or Shakespeare or a kids' play—and nobody paid a dime to be there.

The Miller Outdoor Theatre sits on 7.5 acres and has a 110-ton air conditioner cooling the stage for performers, a $1.5 million sound system, 1,705 seats under a large canopy for those who don't want the lawn experience, aisle lighting, fans over the seats,

While the current stage with its peaked roof was built in 1968, the Miller's original Greek proscenium-style building first opened back in 1923. Bits of it are still around. Hopefully this is the last Miller because nobody should be forced to have more than a few Millers.

 UNIQUE EVENTS AND DESTINATIONS

manicured grounds, and more. It gets millions of dollars' worth of improvements every few years. Around 4,500 people can gather around on lawn chairs or blankets. This is more than enough seats, as typically the mosquitoes carry away stragglers like the scene in the *Wizard of Oz* with the flying monkeys.

But despite the need for bug spray, the performances are amazing, ranging from upscale to family-friendly. Past shows have included a Vivaldi vs. Paganini smackdown; one of the first regionally produced, large-scale, Bollywood musicals; Always...Patsy Cline; the River Oaks Chamber Orchestra; Pinocchio; Cinderella in Spain; a show by some of China's top dance companies; The Dancin' in the Street Motown & More Revue; and classic musicals such as *Anything Goes* and *Mamma Mia!* as well as Movies at the Miller screenings ranging from *Poltergeist* to *Crazy Rich Asians*.

The Miller Outdoor Theatre's distinctive roof is made of three triangular pieces of Corten Steel, which intentionally develops a rusted appearance when exposed to the elements.

What's with Freedom Over Texas?

Every big US city has a nice Fourth of July celebration, and many of them look the same. Alright, New York City has the Statue of Liberty, fireworks cruises, and Nathan's Hot Dogs—it's all good. But nobody does Independence Day quite like Houston's Freedom Over Texas celebration.

Freedom Over Texas is held at Eleanor Tinsley and Sam Houston Parks, a spot that's renowned for having a beautiful view of downtown. Official events run from 4 p.m. until 10 p.m., but people generally start showing up to the area early to claim parking and get a jump on the crowd. And it's a big crowd: around 40,000. The event is also televised.

There are four different concert stages, including a main stage for headliners and a stage just for the kids. Concerts go on for hours, including bands that play classic rock, blues, Tejano, country, zydeco, and more (and a DJ to get that dance vibe going). They try to mix it up so that there's something for everyone, with dozens of acts. There's cold beer and tons of food, jet flyovers, games, contests, chilling in lawn chairs, patriotic music, and all kinds of other cool stuff. Then, of course, the whole thing is capped off with around $100,000 worth of fireworks that light up the sky like we're having a battle with space aliens.

 UNIQUE EVENTS AND DESTINATIONS

Fact BOX

Check the forecast. The year after Harvey, a Texas-sized downpour closed roads, canceled the concerts, and just about washed the whole celebration into the Gulf. Didn't wash away our freedom, though.

Of course, many people forgo the park to watch fireworks from all over town—on rooftops, balconies, patios, in other parks or just stopped on the side of the road. And Freedom Over Texas isn't even the only fireworks show in town. Many suburbs and several neighborhoods within Houston have displays of their own. It's a great day to be an American and a terrible day to be a dog (please bring your dogs inside).

Please remember that Freedom Over Texas provides the fireworks, and only bad things can happen if you light your own in the city. Photo courtesy of Stephanie McCabe on Unsplash.

Like DOMESTIC BEER?

Behold the Beer Can House

Many folks have a passion for home improvement, and John Milkovisch was one of them. Retired from his job at the Southern Pacific railroad, he started decorating his lawn and patio with concrete and other creative found materials in 1968: colorful marbles, interesting rocks, cool redwood, and other accents. And, while he worked, he loved drinking a nice cold beer in the Texas heat. Soon he'd taken care of the lawn, and turned his attention to the house. That's when he realized that he was creating his own

Ripley's Believe It or Not estimated that 50,000 cans were used in the making of the Beer Can House.

construction materials in the form of empty beer cans—and a Houston landmark had begun.

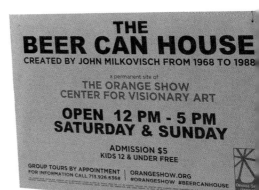

Today this kitschy casa is the ultimate "domestic beer," sporting more than 50,000 empty beer cans. Every bit of the home is covered in beer cans, parts of beer cans, or other unusual materials. The fence and bits of fence post sport beer cans. A garland of beer can tops hangs from the roofline. Beer bottles are set into concrete. Beer cans cover the walls, garage, mailbox, and patio overhang—cans, cans, and more cans. He didn't have some master plan; just drank 'em down and stuck 'em somewhere. And he was brand agnostic, too, buying whatever was on sale.

Today, the Beer Can House is a not-for-profit museum run by The Orange Show Center for Visionary Arts. During regular hours, you can tour the house, hear all about its history, and even check out a collection of classic beer cans on display. The house is on Malone Street in the Rice Military neighborhood east of Memorial Park, between Washington Avenue and Memorial Drive. Admission is just five bucks, leaving you plenty of money for a cheap six-pack of your own.

Fact BOX

How much beer is that? Around 50,000 beer cans were used in the house at 12 ounces per. That's 600,000 ounces or more than 4,867 gallons of brew.

Would anyone else like to say a few words?

The National Museum of Funeral History

How do different cultures ritualize the passing of their people? What happens when a Pope dies? What did old hearses look like? Where can I get a copy of a celebrity death certificate? You can answer all these questions and more at the National Museum of Funeral History.

Some people are scared or uncomfortable by the prospect of visiting a place that's built around death. But if you can get over that initial unease and come to this place with an open mind, it's a fascinating experience. I mean, it happens to everyone, so, you know, don't act like you don't have a dog in this hunt.

It was started by Robert L. Waltrip, who founded Service Corporation International. That company name might not mean anything to you because they keep a low profile, but it is North America's largest provider of funeral home and cemetery

The Museum treats the process of death and bereavement with unfailing respect and reverence. Halloween, however, is a different matter, so check out its annual haunted house.

 UNIQUE EVENTS AND DESTINATIONS

services—owning more than 1,900 in 44 states and eight Canadian provinces. Waltrip knew all there was to know about the business and how it works, and he wanted to share his knowledge with others in the industry, as well as the general public.

You'll find all kinds of permanent exhibits, including those covering:

- The history of cremation
- The history of embalming
- Day of the dead
- Japanese funerals
- 19th-century mourning
- Presidential funerals
- Coffins and caskets of the past
- Historical hearses
- Fantasy coffins from Ghana
- Rare funeral artifacts on display
- A whole bunch more

And, because it's Houston, they even have a recently installed George H. W. Bush Memorial Exhibit honoring the 41st President of the United States. This is the kind of place you just have to wander around to appreciate. It also has a cool gift shop with books, funny T-shirts, spiritual and funereal souvenirs, and more.

So there's a speakeasy for Tex-Mex?

No knock, no nachos at the Last Concert

The Last Concert Cafe at 1403 Nance is the most high-profile low-profile place in town. When you walk up to the joint, there's just a big red door and a painted mural featuring Frida Kahlo. You have to knock, then someone lets you in. Once inside, you can tap into modestly priced plates of Tex-Mex on a generous patio that's perfect for a sunny day. And at night, the place transforms into a concert venue for an eclectic variety of acts that include country, blues, rock, ska, punk, reggae, folk, bluegrass, and more.

As I wrote in my previous book, *Secret Houston*, I used to think that this was just a cute marketing gimmick. The knock, however, has a storied past. The manager told me the place used to be a bordello. If you walk up to that door, you'll notice a little vertical window. Back in the day, they kept that door locked to make sure you weren't a cop; that window was so they could check you out. Inside they hosted nickel dances in the courtyard so you could find your, uh, partner. Then things would progress to the back rooms (I've been back there, and they're just storage now).

In 1949, the place went legit and now claims to be Houston's oldest concert venue. It's a local legend and was even featured in Larry McMurtry's classic novel *Terms of Endearment*. Today it's a colorful place for family, friends, and coworkers to unwind with

 UNIQUE EVENTS AND DESTINATIONS

some live music in the warehouse district. In 2019, a heavy-hitting group of entrepreneurs, restaurateurs, and investors stepped in and gave longtime owner Dawn Fudge the muscle for a number of upgrades and some extra support.

Fact BOX

Some of the buildings comprising the Last Concert Cafe date back to 1860! It's designated a Protected Landmark by the City of Houston, which is saying something since we don't protect much.

The Last Concert's former life as a bordello means you have to knock before someone lets you in.

Are there really ghosts at La Carafe?

This downtown haunt has a chill atmosphere

La Carafe opened in 1860 as a bakery, founded by an Irishman named John Kennedy. It had great bread and terrible timing, as the War Between the States was just kicking off. A clever businessperson, Kennedy transitioned into baking for Confederate soldiers. Across almost a century, the building became, among other things, the Kennedy Trading Post, a Pony Express location back when that was a thing, a drugstore, and a hair salon. It opened as a bar in 1950 and, amazingly, remained in the Kennedy family until 1970.

This is a long, narrow, low-key place with dim lighting and a good wine list. Candles sit on the tables, and two ginormous wax stalagmites grow from burned candles on either side of an antique cash register. Artwork and old photos line the walls. La Carafe has a lot of old-school charm. There is no website. They do not accept credit cards. It has a jukebox with an eclectic selection of chill music. Oh and, of course, ghosts.

Some people have reported seeing ghosts at La Carafe supposedly waiting around for their wagon to arrive, a throwback from when the building was a stagecoach station.

 UNIQUE EVENTS AND DESTINATIONS

Opening as a bakery in 1860, La Carafe is the city's oldest commercial building still in use.

Said to be the most haunted place in town by people purporting to know such things, a number of ghostly apparitions have been reported. One gentleman supposedly felt a tap on his shoulder while in the men's room; turning around, he saw former Idaho Republican Senator Larry Craig! No, just kidding, he didn't see anyone. Then he took off as if escaping a fire. Others have reported seeing a ghostly woman upstairs, a little boy bouncing a ball, a former employee named Carl, and other paranormal strangeness.

Honestly, if you think about some of the people you've met in a bar, someone who makes the air cool and just stares at you quietly in a kind of spooky way wouldn't be the worst drinking buddy.

La Carafe was entered into the National Register of Historic Places in 1979.

Who is Mattress Mack, anyway?

New England has the Kennedy family. Hollywood has Tom Hanks. In H-Town, we've got Jim "Mattress Mack" McIngvale, hard-charging entrepreneur and hero to both the business community and the community at large. McIngvale is the founder of Gallery Furniture—a local furniture empire with three enormous stores and a work ethic that would shame a Midwest farmer.

Not long out of college, McIngvale got a job at a furniture store. He worked hard, but he also paid careful attention. In 1981, with just $5,000 and a vision, McIngvale opened a Houston-area store of his own. He reinvested profits, dreamed big, pushed all his chips into the center of the table, and marketed like a madman. He even wore a mattress in his fast-talking TV commercials, hammering home same-day delivery and his now famous promise to "save you money!"

Today the McIngvales are worth hundreds of millions of dollars. He's got a five-car garage for his Ferrari collection. Along the way, he erected the "World's Largest Christmas Tree," financed a Chuck Norris movie, and co-wrote a book. Yet to this day, you'll find Jim McIngvale working seven days a week at his stores, starring in his own TV commercials, and supporting other local businesspeople.

 LOCAL LEGENDS

McIngvale delivers free in the Houston area with a purchase of $500 or more.

But it's not about his store or money. Houston has many millionaires and more than its share of billionaires (about 13 as of one recent count). H–Town loves McIngvale because he's been there for this city.

His philanthropy seems boundless. He's furnished more than 500 homes for families in need. He donated enormous amounts of money and furniture during Harvey, and even housed refugees personally. McIngvale furnished the teachers' lounges in hundreds of area schools and is always one of the Houston Rodeo's biggest contributors. He's committed millions to hospitals, charities, and institutions of all kinds. As the man himself says: "Why work so hard if you can't do something positive with what you earn?"

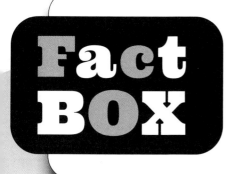

Fact BOX

"I think one of the things that a lot of the citizens in this country miss is the joy of work. Work is life's greatest therapy. In this country, when you meet somebody, you don't ask them this or that, you ask them what you do. Work defines us in this country." —Jim McIngvale

Why is H-E-B our grocery store of record?

For many, there is only one store in town

From Miami to Seattle, stores are stores: the $1.2 million sack of smug, organic produce at Whole Foods or Big Gulps at 7-11, all the same. So it's hard for newcomers to understand the fierce loyalty Houstonians have for San Antonio-based grocery store chain H-E-B.

The unusual name H-E-B stands for Howard Edward Butt—OK, I know, giggle and get it out of your system. The store has a market cap of $20 billion, though, so how's that for a punch line? The Butt family started in 1905 with a $60 loan and a small store in Kerrville. As a boy, Howard Butt delivered groceries with a wagon and went on to champion the store while mastering disintermediation, supply chain optimization, and retail essentials. Today the company has 340 stores and more than 100,000 employees.

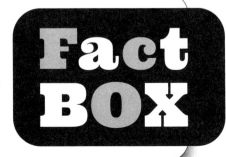

H-E-B: Has Everyone's Back. During Harvey, H-E-B wrestled statewide logistical challenges like a *jiujitsu* master to keep the store a source of calm and plenty—even mobilizing H-E-B water trucks and mobile kitchens.

Fact BOX

LOCAL LEGENDS

So why do Houstonians love it so much? First, it's a Texas thing, and from Texas-shaped pecan pies to homemade tortillas they're all about Texas culture. Second, they buy local. You can get watermelons from a farm outside of town or *pico de gallo* made by a small, local producer. They tailor inventory and store layouts for each location. The employees are usually super helpful and not moping around like they hate life. And each part of the store does its job really well.

I wrote this in the middle of the spring COVID-19 quarantine. If you need groceries, you could have just parked and walked into a Randalls, Kroger, Whole Foods, or Trader Joe's to buy whatever without waiting. But there are ZERO parking spaces in front of my H-E-B. There is a line out the door. Those people can go anywhere and get groceries. But they don't want to go anywhere. This is Houston, so they want to go to H-E-B.

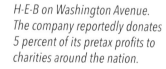

H-E-B on Washington Avenue. The company reportedly donates 5 percent of its pretax profits to charities around the nation.

How come everyone thinks 99 is so great?

Let's face it, even if you love the NFL, it's not always easy to like some of the players and the sketchy things they sometimes do: drug charges, dog fighting, playing for the Cowboys, and so on. But there's one guy H-Town sure likes: J. J. Watt.

As a defensive end, Justin James Watt is a quarterback's worst nightmare. Cause a fumble? Vicious sack? Ha! If you're lucky. Watt's likely to walk an opposing QB out of the stadium, sit him down in the quarterback's overpriced car, start it for him, and give him directions back home. A Wisconsin native, he skipped his senior year at the University of Wisconsin to sign as a first-round draft pick for the Houston Texans in 2011. And a number of opposing players haven't slept well since.

But as savage as he is on field, he's a great guy in the real world. And in this town, he walks on water (or maybe Topo Chico since it's Houston). A young superstar with the world at his feet, he's been the center of no big scandals. No Johnny Manziel–like controversies, no "Do You Know Who I Am?" moments or sketchy legal problems—just hard work and a good attitude.

 LOCAL LEGENDS

Fact BOX

In high school, Watt averaged 13.6 points per game in basketball and held the school shot put record. Who held the record before him? His Dad.

When Hurricane Harvey wrecked the city, Watt created a fund that raised $37M for victims and ultimately built more than 1,183 homes, rebuilt 983 childcare centers, and distributed 283 million meals. Know who asked him to do all that? Nobody. His Justin J. Watt Foundation supports athletic programs at middle schools in Texas and Wisconsin. And he and his wife, soccer star Kealia Ohai Watt, recently gave $350,000 to the Houston Food Bank for victims of COVID-19. Every time you turn around, he's either working overtime or helping overtime.

Watt may have 96 sacks, but I've got 99 socks— so I've got that going for me. Pick yours up at Academy today.

So if you're wondering why Houston loves #99 so much, it's because we love it when the good guys win.

What was AstroWorld, anyway?

Nostalgia for this theme park is widespread

Built in 1968, AstroWorld was a local theme park just across the South Loop from the Astrodome. Many a Houstonian spent their childhood braving rides such as the Texas Cyclone, Greezed Lightnin', or the Thunder River Rapids ride. They could also catch a concert or maybe a Chinese acrobat troupe at the park's Showcase Theatre, walk around eating snow cones or nachos, try to win that giant Tweety Bird playing some space-themed carnival game, or, for the older kids, try even harder to get a date.

AstroWorld was the brainchild of "Judge" Roy Hofheinz, a former Houston mayor among other things, who conceived of and built the Astrodome, as well as AstroWorld, an AstroWorld Hotel, and an additional convention center known as the AstroHall. Altogether the complex was known as the "Astrodomain," billed

Fact BOX

When the park was still going, an AstroWorld T-shirt was the kind of thing you'd wear washing your car. Today, people covet original and reproduction AstroWorld gear like crazy.

 LOCAL LEGENDS

as "The World's Largest and Most Unique Entertainment and Convention Complex."

In the mid-1970s, Hofheinz started having money problems and sold AstroWorld to Six Flags. Six Flags changed hands a few times, and in 2005, it decided to sell off the park to pay down some debt. It was a bad deal for everyone. Though promised $150M, they ended up getting only $77M. And while many proposed theme parks promised to be Houston's next AstroWorld, nothing ever really replaced it. And for generations like me raised going there, nothing ever could. For years now, Houston Rodeo attendees have been using the land as a parking lot.

So get used to hearing people lament Houston's biggest fun-park-turned-parking-lot, making references today's kids could never quite appreciate in the real world. If you want the Six Flags experience, you're looking at a drive to either San Antonio or Arlington. Still, rapper Travis Scott named an album after AstroWorld. So we've got that going for us.

Photographers used to take your picture having fun at the park and then sell you these little keychains with your pic inside. This bridge used to lead over the Loop and into Astroworld. Now it just leads into an empty field.

Is BEYONCÉ really from here?

Beyoncé isn't just a woman; she's a machine. A global celebrity, native Houstonian Beyoncé Giselle Knowles is one of the most influential recording artists to ever come out of H-Town. A driven creative professional and savvy businessperson, she's packed stadiums from Milan to Minneapolis—and it all started right here in Houston.

Knowles went to Elsik High School, as well as the Kinder High School for the Performing and Visual Arts. She started the group that would become Destiny's Child with her cousin and a couple of her classmates in 1990. By 1999 they'd signed with Columbia and soon thereafter went platinum with hits like "Say My Name," "Survivor," and a whole bunch more. If that's all she'd ever done, it would have been more than most musicians could ever hope to accomplish in a lifetime.

But after Destiny's Child flamed out, she went on to release her first solo album, *Dangerously in Love* in 2003. And again she set the world on fire with millions of albums sold and five Grammy Awards. "Single Ladies (Put a Ring on It)" practically broke the Internet. Along the way, she starred in movies, performed for the Obamas, modeled, created her own clothing line, and went on several world tours.

These days, Beyoncé is worth a cool $400 million. She bought her husband (Jay-Z, maybe you've heard of him) a $40 million

 LOCAL LEGENDS

Left: *Beyoncé attended the Kinder High School for the Performing and Visual Arts, one of the nation's most prestigious high schools for creative endeavors.* Right: *Beyonce has been known to hit B&B Butchers on Washington Avenue from time to time while she's in town. So hit 'em up and maybe you'll see her. If not, hey, the steak is still great.*

jet. But she also gives back, both individually and through her BeyGOOD Foundation. She recently teamed up with Twitter's Jack Dorsey to donate $6M in support of mental health and coronavirus–related causes. Despite her status as music industry goddess, she still pops up at her favorite H-Town haunts from time to time.

Fact BOX

"I can never be safe; I always try and go against the grain. As soon as I accomplish one thing, I just set a higher goal. That's how I've gotten to where I am." —Beyoncé Knowles

What's up with the dancing rollerblade guy?

That's how Juan Carlos rolls

If you stop at the intersection of Montrose Boulevard and Allen Parkway, you may just see an enthusiastic man with a stylish haircut on in-line skates dancing like he's at Studio 54 to the approval and delight of drivers and passersby all around. Now, don't mistake this man for the Houston equivalent of one of those street guys in New Orleans who paints himself gold or plays the sax for change in the Quarter. Not only is Juan Carlos a Houston institution who's been cheering up stressed-out commuters for more than 15 years, but he's also a celebrity known nationwide.

Juan Carlos Restrepo was actually born in Medellín, Colombia. Cosmopolitan by nature, Juan Carlos moved to the United States and flitted around a bit in places like New York and Miami before settling in Houston in 1989. His childhood wasn't great. But one thing that always brought him joy was roller skating and listening to music. So when he had time off from his job, Juan Carlos would cruise around his Montrose home getting a little exercise while also getting his groove on, cutting loose, and just being Juan Carlos.

His joy is infectious, especially for the stressed-out folks sitting in rush-hour traffic. You can't help but feel good when he's doing his thing, reminding you that whatever's going on, you shouldn't forget to be happy. Shouldn't forget to be yourself. He's

 LOCAL LEGENDS

been covered by every media outlet around. People wave, honk, and stop to take his picture and get his autograph. If you see him and want to chat, though, be mindful of holding up traffic. Find a place to park and walk to him; he worries about being the cause of traffic problems because it's the opposite of the feeling he wants to give people.

Juan Carlos got into rollerblading as a kid, and today it's made him a national celebrity. So show some love when you drive by. Photo courtesy of Ambroise Nicole via Unsplash.

What was so great about THE ASTRODOME?

Houston still loves the 'dome

Outsiders see the Astrodome as merely an obsolete domed stadium with a larger and more modern replacement already in play, because what's the big deal about a big indoor sports arena? Don't they have them everywhere? Well, that's the thing: the Astrodome was the first.

Dubbed the "Eighth Wonder of the World," it was the world's first fully enclosed, air-conditioned multipurpose sports arena. Roy "The Judge" Hofheinz championed the project, simultaneously bringing a Major League Baseball (MLB) team to Houston. Ground was broken in 1962. Houston's first MLB team was tentatively called the Colt .45s. At the Astrodome's groundbreaking, .45 revolvers were shot into the soil as an inauguration. The Colt .45s played in a temporary stadium nearby

Fact BOX

Traditional grass wouldn't grow in the Astrodome's enclosed environment. So the 'stros brought in a synthetic Monsanto product called ChemGrass, which was rebranded as "AstroTurf" thereafter in honor of the Astrodome.

 LOCAL LEGENDS

called Colt Stadium until changing their name to the Houston Astros and playing their first game in the 'dome on April 9, 1965. It was an exhibition game against the Yankees; President Johnson attended. After the Astrodome opened, Colt Stadium was taken apart and shipped to Mexico.

So the Astrodome basically pioneered indoor sports, and we have a real soft spot for the historic old building. Recent years haven't been kind now that we have Minute Maid Park and NRG Stadium. The 'dome was relegated to C-List events, and in 2008, it failed to pass a fire inspection. Eventually, it was targeted for demolition. Seats and other memorabilia were stripped and auctioned. Bits of it were destroyed, including its ramp towers. A $217M restoration bond failed to pass in 2013. Things were looking up in 2018 when a $105M revitalization initiative was passed by Harris County. However, since the election of a new county judge, all plans to restore or transform the historic building ground to a halt. Hopefully the facility gets another chance at bat sometime soon.

The Astrodome was the world's first air-conditioned dome stadium. Fun fact: In later years, a man lived in the 'dome whose job was to take care of the feral cats brought in to hunt the rats which had become a problem at some point. So he literally herded cats. Photo by Carol M. Highsmith, courtesy of the Library of Congress.

The Bush family legacy is everywhere.

George H. W. and Barbara Bush moved to Texas in the late 1940s to join in the "awl bidniss." And, like many people in that industry, they eventually found their way to Houston to make the most of their interests. After a long and distinguished career in public service, culminating in his term as the 41st president of the United States, Bush came home to his adopted hometown and played a big role in the community.

The president kept an office on Memorial Drive, and the family lived in West Oaks, where they lived a quiet life of service and philanthropy. This is Texas, but it's also a large and diverse city, so not everybody in town appreciated his conservative politics. But everybody appreciated the family's generosity and support for countless charities ranging from literacy to cancer research—and for the community in general. But don't take my word; just look around town for the Bush name.

First off, Sesquicentennial Park downtown sports an eight-foot

George H. W. Bush Monument at Franklin and Bagby downtown in Sesquicentennial Park

 LOCAL LEGENDS

bronze statue of George H. W. Bush, surrounded by four *bas-reliefs* featuring Bush as a US Navy pilot, an oilman, a diplomat, and a father attending the inauguration of George W. Bush as the 43rd president. The city's largest airport is named George Bush Intercontinental Airport. Oh, and there's a high school in the Houston suburb of Richmond named after 41. A Harris County Public Library is named after Barbara Bush. There's even a Millie Bush Dog Park in far west Houston. And just up the road is the George H. W. Bush Presidential Library at Texas A&M University in College Station. So the family's legacy is tough to miss in these parts.

Millions in the Houston area mourned the couple's eventual passing, Barbara in April 2018 and George H. W. in November 2018.

George W. Bush speaking at Johnson Space Center. Photo courtesy of History in HD via Unsplash.

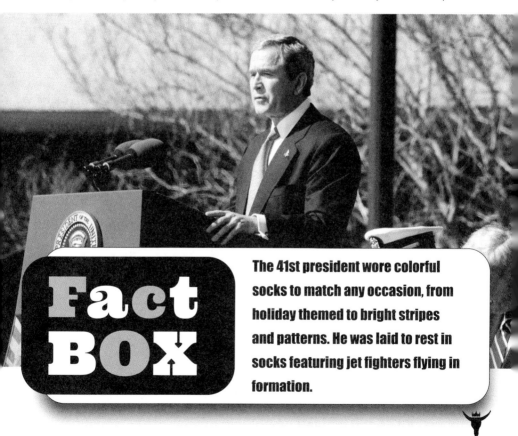

Fact BOX

The 41st president wore colorful socks to match any occasion, from holiday themed to bright stripes and patterns. He was laid to rest in socks featuring jet fighters flying in formation.

Who the @&#! was *Sam Houston?*

Hero of the Texas Revolution

Sam Houston, among many other things, led the army of the Republic of Texas to victory against Mexican military leader General Antonio López de Santa Anna at the Battle of San Jacinto in 1836. A larger-than-life character, he was the perfect namesake for the city that would arise in the battle's shadow not a decade later.

Much like his namesake city, Sam Houston was big, bold, and full of surprises. Born in Virginia, he moved to Tennessee as a boy. He periodically went to live with the Cherokee people who gave him the nickname *Colonneh* or the Raven. Injured fighting the British during the War of 1812, he studied law and was elected to the US House of Representatives for the state of Tennessee. He often dressed as a Cherokee. In Washington, he

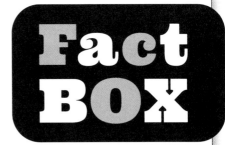

How did Sam Houston win the Texas Revolution? He retreated continually, buying time for proper training. When finally pinned, he launched a surprise attack during the enemy's afternoon siesta that obliterated Santa Anna's forces in just 18 minutes.

 LOCAL LEGENDS

beat an Ohio representative with his cane over a perceived insult. Eventually, Houston became the governor of Tennessee.

In 1832, Houston came to Texas, which Mexico had recently wrested from Spain. The Mexican government had opened up the Texas frontier to colonization, and Houston had moved down ostensibly to engage in land speculation and serve as a Cherokee liaison. Some suspect he was actually an *agent provocateur* for the US government to foment rebellion. If that was indeed the case, it worked—Texas became its own nation, with Houston as its president.

He couldn't succeed himself by law, so after his first term, he served as a Texas Congressman in San Augustine from 1839 to 1841 (my father was actually born in what used to be his law office). Then he became the nation's third president. Texas was annexed into the United States in 1845, and Houston became its governor in 1859— making him the only person to ever be the governor of two different states.

Why do people keep talking about "slime in the ice machine"?

Living in Houston, you'll eventually hear the phrase: "Slime in the ice machine." This is an allusion to longtime television personality and investigative journalist Marvin Harold Zindler Sr., who for decades delivered a health inspection segment on Houston's restaurants for ABC KTRK TV Channel 13. His segments appeared along with the evening news, and he reported restaurants failing various aspects of inspection such as which places had rats, which kept food off-temperature, and so forth. Part of the show revealed who had slime in the ice machine, which became a catchphrase over the years. In 1988, he signed a lifetime contract to do the segment and worked right up to his passing in 2007 at age 85.

"Slime in the ice machine" made Zindler famous, but he was much more than a TV personality. He'd been a radio DJ, a cop, a US Marine, a photographer for the *Houston Press*, and an employee of the Harris County Sheriff's Department in the 1960s. In the early 1970s, he went to work for KTRK and stayed—a post that resulted in groundbreaking investigations and took him around the world.

He's known nationally for shutting down the now-infamous Chicken Ranch brothel in La Grange, Texas. Institutions of ill repute had been going for 100+ years in La Grange. One in particular, which was founded around 1905, catered to businessmen

LOCAL LEGENDS

Marvin Zindler's health and safety restaurant report made famous the phrase "Slime in the ice machine!"

and politicians. During the Great Depression food was scarce, so the place instituted a "one chicken, one [er . . .] visit," policy that earned it the moniker of Chicken Ranch. Zindler, whose real problem with the place was its ties to organized crime, routed the "ranch" in a week-long exposé. It closed the next week. A few years later, two Houston lawyers bought the ranch, moving part of the building to Dallas and promoting it as a chicken joint called the "Chicken Ranch."

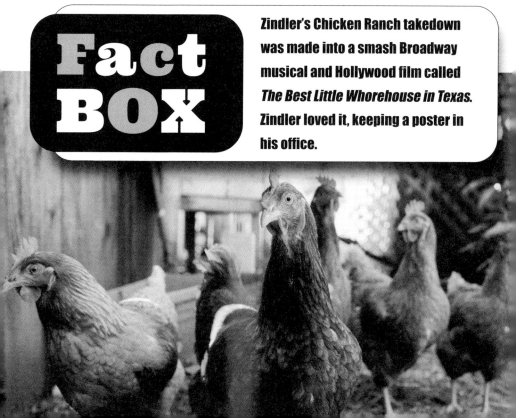

Fact BOX

Zindler's Chicken Ranch takedown was made into a smash Broadway musical and Hollywood film called *The Best Little Whorehouse in Texas.* Zindler loved it, keeping a poster in his office.

Who was Dr. Red Duke?

This legendary doctor's legacy is still saving lives

Houston has no shortage of medical heroes, some still practicing and others relegated to history. But one of its most beloved is the late Dr. James H. "Red" Duke Jr. (1928–2015). A trauma surgeon at both the University of Texas Health Science Center and the

Dr. Red Duke pioneered the Life Flight program at Memorial Hermann hospital.

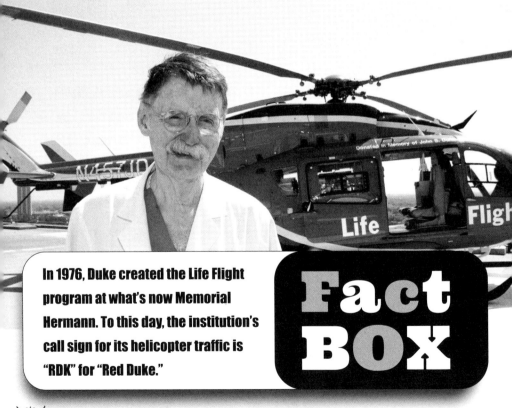

In 1976, Duke created the Life Flight program at what's now Memorial Hermann. To this day, the institution's call sign for its helicopter traffic is "RDK" for "Red Duke."

Fact BOX

 LOCAL LEGENDS

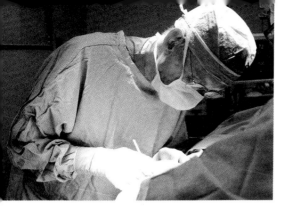

Dr. Red Duke was known to play country music in the surgical theater.

Memorial Hermann hospital system, Dr. Red Duke helped keep Houston healthy for decades as both a medical leader and educator. Duke was in the Corps at A&M, went to divinity school, and felt a calling to serve the community through the practice of medicine. He graduated from med school in Dallas just in time to help save the life of Texas Governor John Connally in the wake of the Kennedy assassination in 1963.

Duke had a bushy moustache, thick Texas accent, and penchant for chewing tobacco. He was known to play country music in the operating room—all while performing the most technically complex surgeries, saving people who were considered beyond hope, teaching others along the way, and working tirelessly. He once engaged in a 50+ hour surgery on a constable who'd been shot. Can you imagine performing a surgery that lasted 2+ days?

A peerless innovator, mentor, and educator, Duke would often ask new doctors who the most important person in the operating theater is; if they said the surgeon, rather than the patient, a lengthy lecture ensued. And he was so charismatic that TV was a perfect fit. His "Dr. Red Duke Texas Health Reports" aired regionally, enabling him to dole out homespun health, medical, and wellness advice. All of Texas loved him, and despite his passing in 2015, his work continues to touch generations of Houstonians.

Do we really get big-city living on the cheap?

If you have enough money, practically any city can be a great place to live, even Dallas. But most people have to crunch the numbers to decide if a city's balance of costs versus opportunity or earning potential makes sense for them. In terms of living costs, Houston offers a lot of the big city perks at a price that's pretty sweet when viewed on a global or national scale.

The *Houston Business Journal* reports that a recent study ranked H-Town the 39th most affordable city in the nation (San Francisco ranked 75th out of the 75 cities assessed). It's cheaper to live here than either Dallas or Austin. And you still get big city opportunities, such as the chance to make new friends during an unexpected home-invasion style robbery. Just kidding, there are a lot of upsides to city life, even now.

It's more expensive than it used to be. Still, according to Zillow the average home value in Houston is $191,907. That's $141 per square foot, with an average list price of $283,000. The average rent house costs $1,500, and the average apartment rents at around $1,118. Out of 472 cities around the world, Houston ranked as the 117th most affordable. The Top 5 most expensive cities in the world are all in Switzerland; the sixth is New York.

 HOUSTONIANS AT HOME

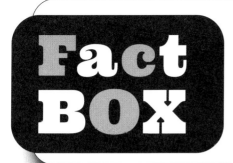

Fact BOX

Check out expatistan.com for comparisons of how the costs of basic goods and services in Houston and other cities stack up. The site lists the common costs of homes, cars, food, theater tickets, and more.

Now, the caveat is transportation. Texas Monthly recently reported HUD data that said while Houston's monthly median housing costs were $400 lower than NYC, factoring in median transportation costs meant it was only around $79 cheaper. Still, the average list price for a house in Manhattan is approximately $1,550,000. The average list price in Bern, Switzerland is $1.2 million easy. So I think I'll stick with good old H-Town, thank you very much.

Houston's cost of living is 2 percent lower than the national average, offering big city living that's actually doable for most. Photo courtesy of Matt Wang via Unsplash.

How important is AIR-CONDITIONING here?

"Air-Conditioning Capital of the World"

Air-conditioning is life here in Houston. On average, Houston is hotter than Death Valley. And the humidity is like a horror movie in which a madman has turned a giant steam sauna on its highest setting and locked the door from the outside.

To compensate, homes, offices, stores, and other buildings are air conditioned like walk-in fish coolers. Any office worker with a body mass index of 40 or below brings a sweater to work in August despite tar melting on the road outside. Menopausal women simply set the thermostat as low as possible at bedtime, instructing spouses and children to build campfires from bits of furniture should they get cold.

The first modern air-conditioning unit was built in 1902 by Willis Carrier; you can still buy a Carrier air conditioner. The problem he was trying to solve was keeping paper from

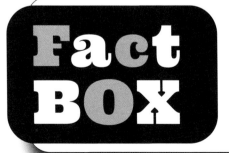

Fact BOX

Nobody wants to walk four blocks in 95-degree weather with 90 percent humidity for a hot lunch. That's why 20-feet beneath downtown you'll find air-conditioned tunnels connecting 95 city blocks.

 HOUSTONIANS AT HOME

Houston is often billed as the "Air-Conditioning Capital of the World."

wrinkling at a Brooklyn lithography and publishing company. But what he ended up doing was preventing future Southerners from simply spending all day sitting buck naked in a hammock drinking Chiltons.

Movie theaters were among the first to install air-conditioning, and for decades, many a Houstonian paid not so much for the film as for a chance to sit in the cool. Opening in 1941, the Millie Esperson building downtown was the first air-conditioned high-rise. Air-conditioning was a luxury available only to wealthy Houstonians in its earliest days. But today, people will sacrifice a lot before they sacrifice the relief of cool, dry

air on demand. So get used to going between extreme heat and cold when you go about your day.

Pro tip: Houston air conditioners work hard. Invest in a good one if you can, change air filters regularly, and have an air-conditioning company come out once a year for preventive maintenance.

The Wells Fargo Plaza entrance to downtown's extensive network of air-conditioned tunnels.

Why are there no basements here?

Sorry, bro, that man cave needs to go elsewhere

I was always jealous of my Northern and Midwestern friends who have basements—often decked out with pool tables, fully stocked bars, or home theater systems. Sadly, we have plenty of man caves but very few basements in people's houses. And there are a few reasons.

First off, as becomes tragically evident every once in a while, Houston is close to sea level. That means you start digging and hit water in as little as six feet. In the past when putting in a new fence, I've not bothered adding water to mixed concrete when digging a fence post—because water naturally just ran into the hole. This zone of water saturation near the soil's surface is known as the water table. And it means if you put a basement in a Houston home it will likely flood. So that's the major reason.

Another reason is the type of soil we have down here. Houston's clay soil has expansive properties; it shrinks and swells with moisture, making the simple maintenance of a home's slab foundation difficult, let alone a basement. Take it from someone who's spent tens of thousands of dollars on foundation-related repairs, Houston soil makes each of us more boat captains than homeowners.

Also, there's our warm weather to consider. Up North, they have to build down past the frost line so extreme cold doesn't cause

 **HOUSTONIANS AT HOME**

problems with piping and such. If you're already digging so deep, it doesn't cost much more to add a basement. But in Houston, frost is just the stuff that forms all over your chilled beer mug. The winter frost line here is something like less than five inches into the soil. So while the odd house or building around town may have a basement, you just don't see them that often.

Basements are something you just don't see much of in Houston or Texas in general. Guess that man cave will have to go elsewhere.

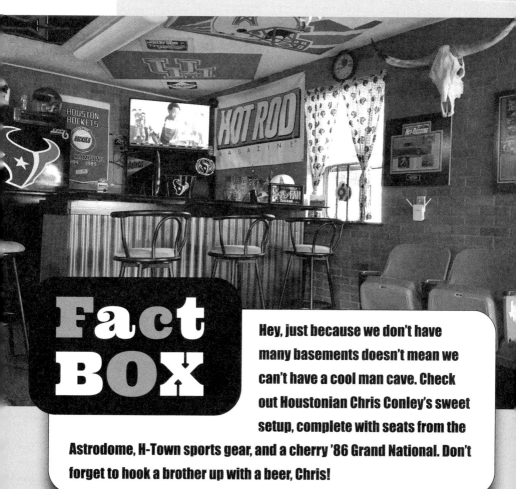

Fact BOX

Hey, just because we don't have many basements doesn't mean we can't have a cool man cave. Check out Houstonian Chris Conley's sweet setup, complete with seats from the Astrodome, H-Town sports gear, and a cherry '86 Grand National. Don't forget to hook a brother up with a beer, Chris!

SOURCES

Diversity
https://www.houstonchronicle.com/news/houston-texas/article/Houstonians-speak-at-least-145-languages-at-home-6613182.php
https://www.youtube.com/watch?v=u8GsQcdQoNY
https://www.houstonchronicle.com/news/houston-texas/houston/article/Harris-County-unveils-multilingual-virtual-15057921.php
https://kinder.rice.edu/sites/g/files/bxs1676/f/documents/Houston%20Region%20Grows%20More%20Ethnically%20Diverse%204-9.pdf
https://www.smithsonianmag.com/travel/what-makes-houston-the-next-great-american-city-4870584/

Dallas Rivalry
https://matadornetwork.com/read/11-differences-houston-dallas-always-cause-arguments/
https://www.dallasnews.com/news/texas/2017/08/30/dallas-vs-houston-rivalry-means-nothing-next-to-the-bond-our-cities-share/
https://www.csmonitor.com/2001/0405/p3s1.html
https://en.wikipedia.org/wiki/Governor%27s_Cup_(Texas)
https://www.reddit.com/r/Dallas/comments/csie8h/whats_the_deal_with_the_houston_rivalry/
https://www.texasmonthly.com/the-daily-post/texass-cities-one-big-dysfunctional-family/
https://www.houston.org/why-houston/industries/energy
https://en.wikipedia.org/wiki/The_Comeback_(American_football)

Loop Life
https://www.houstontx.gov/planning/Demographics/Loop%20610%20Website/
https://www.dailymail.co.uk/news/article-3140595/Bridge-tunnel-added-Oxford-English-Dictionary-defined-unsophisticated.html

http://www.davestravelcorner.com/journals/destination-europe/understanding-london-northsouth-river-thames-divide/
https://en.wikipedia.org/wiki/List_of_United_States_cities_by_area

Gun Culture
https://www.cbsnews.com/pictures/gun-ownership-rates-by-state/34/
https://www.houstonpress.com/news/how-many-texans-own-guns-a-whole-freakin-lot-poll-shows-6720585

High Oil Prices
https://www.texasmonthly.com/energy/evolution-energy-capital-world/
https://www.houston.org/why-houston/industries/energy
https://www.bmmagazine.co.uk/business/why-is-houston-the-energy-capital-of-the-world/
https://www.houstonchronicle.com/business/energy/article/Oil-sector-may-be-entering-final-decade-of-growth-14931374.php

Megachurches
https://www.houstonpress.com/music/what-was-your-favorite-concert-at-the-summit-6497173
https://en.wikipedia.org/wiki/Lakewood_Church_Central_Campus
https://www.chron.com/life/houston-belief/article/Here-are-Texas-biggest-megachurches-6071667.php#photo-4439624
https://kinder.rice.edu/2016/04/25/in-houston-the-land-of-megachurches-fewer-people-attending-religious-services
https://www.cnn.com/2019/04/27/us/what-is-a-megachurch-explainer/index.html
https://www.chron.com/news/investigations/article/How-does-Lakewood-Church-spend-its-millions-We-12955372.php#photo-6478709
https://www.houstoniamag.com/news-and-city-life/2016/03/city-of-faith-religion-in-houston-by-the-numbers
https://www.illuminidol.com/products/james-harden

174

Houston, We Have a Cliché

https://www.newsweek.com/houston-we-have-recipe-whats-cooking-o-169506

https://www.houstonchronicle.com/entertainment/article/why-do-people-say-houston-we-have-a-problem-14518979.php

https://www.wsj.com/articles/houstons-world-series-problem-the-phrase-houston-we-have-a-problem-1509030847

https://www.houstonchronicle.com/local/gray-matters/article/Lisa-Gray-I-have-a-problem-with-Houston-we-12831502.php

https://www.washingtonpost.com/news/retropolis/wp/2017/04/13/houston-we-have-a-problem-the-amazing-history-of-the-iconic-apollo-13-misquote/

https://www.amazon.com/Houston-Have-Prob-Llama-Funny-Space/dp/B07RDS8MMQ

https://www.nasa.gov/johnson/HWHAP

la Quinceañera

https://www.britannica.com/topic/quinceanera

https://www.nytimes.com/2016/06/05/nyregion/the-quinceanera-a-rite-of-passage-in-transition.html

https://www.usatoday.com/story/life/2017/09/09/modern-quinceaneras-add-trends-tradition/645830001/

https://www.washingtonpost.com/local/a-new-american-tradition—the-double-quinceanera/2019/10/24/38b4d940-f59a-11e9-ad8b-85e2aa00b5ce_story.html

https://www.chron.com/life/article/Houston-lavish-quinceanera-goes-all-out-traditions-14091081.php

https://www.khou.com/article/features/houston-teen-invites-her-guests-to-register-to-vote-while-celebrating-her-quinceanera/285-8c7dbec2-fcaa-415a-95f5-4818b766fd46

https://www.chron.com/news/houston-texas/houston/article/Big-business-of-quincea-eras-on-display-at-expo-13565951.php

Warm Winters

https://www.visithoustontexas.com/travel-planning/weather/

https://abc13.com/5798403/

https://www.click2houston.com/weather/2020/01/03/where-is-houstons-winter/

https://www.click2houston.com/news/2017/12/08/houston-hurricanes-and-snowfall-linked-this-is-what-you-need-to-know/

Hurricanes

houstonoem.org

https://spaceplace.nasa.gov/hurricanes/en/

https://www.houstonpublicmedia.org/articles/news/hurricane/2019/07/11/338975/newbies-guide-to-hurricanes-and-storm-prep/

https://www.houstonpublicmedia.org/articles/shows/hurricane-season/2018/07/03/292669/hurricane-season-trailer/

https://www.houstonpress.com/news/hurricane-season-officially-underway-11303221

https://www.click2houston.com/weather/2019/09/20/8-of-the-most-destructive-storms-in-houstons-history/

Flooding

https://slate.com/business/2017/08/how-houston-and-harris-countys-zoning-approach-affected-hurricane-harvey-flooding.html

https://www.houstonpublicmedia.org/news/weather/

houstonoem.org

https://www.houstonchronicle.com/life/article/disaster-expert-houston-hurricane-coronavirus-Q-A-15303083.php

https://www.houstonchronicle.com/life/article/Rain-free-floods-Allergy-season-And-other-15111362.php

Humidity

https://science.howstuffworks.com/nature/climate-weather/atmospheric/question651.htm

https://www.beaumontenterprise.com/photos/article/10-most-humid-cities-in-America-1337274.php#photo-938825

https://www.click2houston.com/weather/2019/11/06/happy-contrails-houston/

https://www.pbs.org/newshour/science/8-things-didnt-know-humidity

https://www.cigaraficionado.com/article/storing-cigars-7429

http://www.saigon.climatemps.com/humidity.php

https://www.mentalfloss.com/article/74148/why-isnt-100-percent-humidity-always-rain

Pollen

https://www.aafa.org/allergy-capitals/

https://www.aafa.org/media/2340/aafa-2019-spring-allergy-capitals-report.pdf

https://www.houstontx.gov/health/Pollen-Mold/

https://pollen.aaaai.org/nab/index.cfm?p=allergenreport&stationid=188

https://www.houstonchronicle.com/business/houston-how-to/article/How-to-navigate-Houston-s-endless-allergy-season-14535846.php#

https://www.chron.com/news/houston-texas/houston/article/Houston-pollen-counts-highest-in-United-States-13709141.php

https://www.click2houston.com/weather/2020/02/28/allergy-sufferers-will-get-hit-hard-this-spring/

https://www.aaaai.org/conditions-and-treatments/library/allergy-library/outdoor-allergens

https://mycology.adelaide.edu.au/descriptions/hyphomycetes/alternaria/

https://www.cdc.gov/fungal/diseases/aspergillosis/index.html

https://mycology.adelaide.edu.au/descriptions/hyphomycetes/cladosporium/

http://www.greenhoustontx.gov/greenspace.html

https://www.texasmonthly.com/the-culture/green-acres-2/

Zoning

https://www.chron.com/news/houston-texas/houston/article/Weirdest-images-from-Houston-s-lack-of-zoning-laws-9171688.php

https://kinder.rice.edu/2015/09/08/forget-what-youve-heard-houston-really-does-have-zoning-sort-of

https://thefederalist.com/2016/05/13/how-no-zoning-laws-works-for-houston/

https://www.architectmagazine.com/design/urbanism-planning/will-houstons-city-plan-transform-this-no-zoning-mecca-karrie-jacobs-investigates_o

https://www.click2houston.com/news/local/2020/02/23/ask-2-does-houston-have-zoning/

https://slate.com/business/2017/08/how-houston-and-harris-countys-zoning-approach-affected-hurricane-harvey-flooding.html

https://www.thezoningresearchgroup.com/post/houston-the-city-without-zoning-five-things-to-know

https://urbanland.uli.org/industry-sectors/city-almost-no-limits/

https://www.dallasnews.com/opinion/commentary/2017/08/31/zoning-would-not-have-saved-houston/

https://www.dartmouth.edu/~wfischel/Papers/02-03.pdf

http://cityobservatory.org/sprawl-beyond-zoning/

https://www.strongtowns.org/journal/2017/6/28/a-history-of-zoning-in-three-acts-part-i

http://www.houstontx.gov/planning/Commissions/commiss_plan.html

Multiple Skylines

https://www.chron.com/news/houston-texas/houston/article/Houston-skyline-s-13330138.php

http://www.chasetower.com/building.php?sect=1

Texas Medical Center

https://www.tmc.edu/about-tmc/

https://www.tmc.edu/wp-content/uploads/2016/08/TMC_FactsFiguresOnePager_0307162.pdf

https://www.mdanderson.org/about-md-anderson/facts-history/who-was-md-anderson.html

https://www.houstonchronicle.com/business/medical/article/Facts-figures-Texas-Medical-Center-TMC-MD-Anderson-12734881.php

https://www.forbes.com/sites/scottbeyer/2015/12/11/the-texas-medical-center-houstons-medical-mini-city/#f9a23b512928

https://www.mdanderson.org/about-md-anderson/facts-history/institutional-profile.html

What Is a Ward?

https://houstonhistorymagazine.org/2011/07/when-there-were-wards-a-series/

https://www.cubesmart.com/blog/city-guides/houston/houston-moving-guide/be-in-the-know-life-in-the-six-wards-of-houston/

https://www.houstontx.gov/planning/HistoricPres/HistoricPreservationManual/historic_districts/high_first_ward.html

https://www.houstonchronicle.com/life/article/Winds-of-change-blow-through-Houston-s-Second-Ward-5544891.php#

https://www.houstonchronicle.com/local/gray-matters/article/houston-third-ward-gentrification-community-trust-12972879.php

https://www.houstoniamag.com/arts-and-culture/2017/11/fourth-ward-houston-photographs-from-1987

https://www.texasmonthly.com/articles/only-the-strong-survive/

http://houstonhistorymagazine.org/wp-content/uploads/2010/12/vol-8-no-1-Ward-Series.pdf

https://www.etymonline.com/word/alderman

https://houstonhistorymagazine.org/wp-content/uploads/2015/09/ward-system-of-government.pdf

https://www.houstonpress.com/arts/the-changing-face-of-houston-the-old-sixth-ward-6384472

https://texashighways.com/culture/art-music/how-houston-s-first-ward-industrial-yard-transformed-into-an-artistic-epicenter/

Transco Tower

https://www.chron.com/news/houston-texas/houston/article/What-is-at-the-top-of-Williams-Tower-12304859.php

http://swamplot.com/shining-a-little-more-light-on-the-williams-tower-beacons-return/2016-02-09/

http://swamplot.com/why-the-williams-tower-beacon-was-off-last-fall/2016-02-05/

https://www.hines.com/about

https://www.houstonarchitecture.com/Building/542/Williams-Tower.php

https://www.emporis.com/buildings/117714/williams-tower-houston-tx-usa

https://www.houstonchronicle.com/business/real-estate/article/412-million-buys-towering-Houston-icon-4331225.php#

https://www.nytimes.com/1995/01/31/business/company-news-williams-companies-to-invest-millions-in-transco.html

https://northeastsupplyenhancement.com/wp-content/uploads/2016/11/transco-fact-sheet.pdf

https://www.forbes.com/sites/larryolmsted/2016/11/04/americas-best-classic-restaurants-21-club-new-york-city/#19df5ccd1e77

https://www.airnav.com/airports/us/TX?type=H&use=R

Taco Wars

https://www.houstoniamag.com/eat-and-drink/2018/03/best-tacos-houston

https://www.houstonchronicle.com/neighborhood/article/The-best-breakfast-tacos-Houston-2019-14828802.php#

https://www.click2houston.com/food/2019/10/04/here-are-12-tacos-you-should-try-in-houston/

https://www.houstonpublicmedia.org/articles/shows/houston-matters/2019/04/04/327641/houstons-best-places-for-tex-mex-and-tacos/

https://www.thrillist.com/eat/houston/the-best-tacos-in-houston

https://www.smithsonianmag.com/arts-culture/where-did-the-taco-come-from-81228162/

https://www.houstoniamag.com/eat-and-drink/2018/03/best-tacos-houston

https://www.thrillist.com/eat/nation/history-of-taco-tuesday-when-did-it-start

Iced Tea

http://www.teausa.com/14655/tea-fact-sheet

https://www.texasmonthly.com/the-daily-post/sweet-tea-line/

https://www.khou.com/article/news/local/the-quest-for-the-best-texas-iced-tea/285-342617914

https://www.dallasnews.com/news/2018/08/29/how-do-texans-make-the-perfect-glass-of-iced-tea/

https://www.houstoniamag.com/eat-and-drink/2016/04/10-drinks-every-houstonian-must-know

https://www.houstonchronicle.com/life/food/article/The-summer-kitchen-s-secret-ingredient-13860677.php#

https://www.theatlantic.com/national/archive/2011/01/where-does-the-south-begin/70052/

Crawfish

https://www.click2houston.com/food/2020/01/30/this-app-will-help-you-find-the-best-crawfish-in-houston/?__vfz=medium%3Dsharebar

https://www.houstonchronicle.com/life/article/The-official-bird-of-Houston-loves-crawfish-just-14467735.php#

http://crazyalanswampshack.com/blog/the-rich-and-tangled-history-of-crawfish-in-houston-texas/

https://www.texasmonthly.com/food/houston-crawfish-invasion/

https://www.khou.com/article/life/food/crawfish-season-11-top-spots-in-houston-area/285-0dc99a6c-cfa2-4412-bb05-48c822f5255e

https://www.houstoniamag.com/eat-and-drink/when-is-crawfish-season

https://www.visithoustontexas.com/restaurants-and-bars/cultural-fare/crawfish-season-in-houston/

https://www.tripsavvy.com/houstons-crawfish-season-4126648

https://www.houston.org/news/houston-population-expected-exceed-71-million-2020

Food Trucks

https://www.thrillist.com/eat/houston/best-food-trucks-in-houston

https://www.visithoustontexas.com/restaurants-and-bars/restaurants-and-eateries/houston-food-trucks/

https://www.houstoniamag.com/eat-and-drink/2019/08/best-food-trucks-in-houston

https://www.houstonchronicle.com/entertainment/dining/article/10-popular-Houston-food-trucks-14981272.php#

https://mobile-cuisine.com/business/history-of-american-food-trucks/

https://www.bizjournals.com/houston/news/2018/03/22/houston-named-no-6-food-truck-city-in-new-report.html

https://www.houstonpress.com/restaurants/a-very-nearly-comprehensive-guide-to-houstons-food-trucks-6404391

https://www.houstonpress.com/restaurants/a-very-nearly-comprehensive-guide-to-houstons-food-trucks-6404391

Food from Far and Wide

https://www.houstonchronicle.com/news/houston-texas/article/Houstonians-speak-at-least-145-languages-at-home-6613182.php

https://www.yelp.com/search?cflt=intlgrocery&find_loc=Houston%2C+TX

http://manenas.com/ourmenu.htm

http://www.ricebowlhouston.com/

http://bluenilerestaurant.com/

https://houston.eater.com/maps/houston-best-indian-pakistani-restaurants

https://www.zagat.com/r/indika-houston

Brewston, Texas

https://www.houstoniamag.com/eat-and-drink/2019/05/best-houston-breweries-local-craft-beer

http://beerchronicle.com/houston-breweries/

https://www.saintarnold.com/seasonal-beers/

https://experience.visithouston.com/checkout/3/visit-houston/415/houston-brew-pass

https://www.karbachbrewing.com/

https://www.chron.com/life/article/Houston-has-a-rich-beer-history-3549574.php

https://www.peachridgeglass.com/2013/11/houston-ice-and-brewing-co-magnolia-brewery/

https://www.heritagesociety.org/magnolia-brewing-building

https://8thwonder.com/distillery

Whataburger

https://www.khou.com/article/news/local/whatawedding-houston-couple-among-6-chosen-to-get-married-renew-vows-at-whataburger/285-5bdc3d66-c4e7-4647-8b1e-61675eb1a595

https://houston.culturemap.com/news/city-life/07-05-19-mad-houston-restautant-reservations-six-weeks-whataburger-sold-bdt-capital-partners-rodeo-carnival/

https://www.chron.com/news/houston-texas/houston/article/Whataburger-sale-idea-JJ-Watt-Houston-Texas-fans-13998697.php

https://www.houstoniamag.com/arts-and-culture/2017/06/houston-loves-whataburger

https://time.com/5612280/whataburger-texas-sale/

https://houston.eater.com/2018/10/12/17968036/beto-orourke-houston-mural-whataburger

https://www.bonappetit.com/restaurants-travel/article/whataburger-history-texas

https://www.vice.com/en_us/article/wn9vb4/why-texas-cant-seem-to-fall-in-love-with-in-n-out-burger

https://www.nytimes.com/2019/06/20/us/texas-whataburger-chicago.html

https://www.houstoniamag.com/eat-and-drink/2019/05/best-burgers-and-beer-in-houston

https://stories.whataburger.com/press-room

https://www.mashed.com/135332/the-untold-truth-of-whataburger/

https://twitter.com/jjwatt/status/1139592784715931648?lang=en

Houston Is an Hour from Houston

https://www.texasmonthly.com/the-daily-post/as-if-you-needed-it-further-proof-that-houston-is-so-much-bigger-than-most-cities/

https://twitter.com/jjwatt/status/1139592784715931648?lang=en

https://www.houstontx.gov/abouthouston/houstonfacts.html

https://kinder.rice.edu/2017/09/21/how-urban-or-suburban-is-sprawling-houston

https://www.mentalfloss.com/article/69534/how-many-cities-can-fit-houston

https://www.houstonchronicle.com/houston/article/See-how-big-the-Grand-

Parkway-is-compared-to-other-6657488.
php#
https://www.houstoniamag.com/
newcomers-guide/2018/08/new-to-
houston-guide
https://tshaonline.org/handbook/online/
articles/hdh03
https://www.houstonchronicle.com/news/
investigations/article/Houston-s-roads-
drivers-are-nation-s-most-12865072.php
https://www.ktsa.com/houston-has-the-
worst-traffic-in-texas-boston-worst-in-u-s/
https://www.houston.org/sites/default/
files/2019-08/Houston%20Facts%20
2019%20Final_3.pdf
https://hogg.utexas.edu/wp-content/upload
s/2018/10/02C20W00120Houston20Area2
0Profile1.pdf

Trucks
https://www.compare.com/auto-insurance/
by-state/texas/popular-texas-cars
https://www.houstonchronicle.com/
business/bizfeed/article/Which-car-models-
last-the-longest-in-Houston-15104508.php
https://www.houstonchronicle.com/
business/bizfeed/article/Houston-s-top-
selling-used-cars-in-2019-14929732.php
https://marker.medium.com/teslas-
cybertruck-has-a-huge-cowboy-problem-
bebe81377c6d
https://patch.com/texas/houston/chevy-
trucks-tops-list-most-stolen-vehicle-houston
https://www.click2houston.com/
news/2019/06/25/stolen-trucks-
believed-to-be-used-for-human-trafficking-
smuggling-liberty-county-officials-say/
https://www.houstonchronicle.com/
business/retail/article/PHOTOS-These-
were-the-best-selling-vehicles-in-13779273.
php
https://store.gilleys.com/products/bud-n-
sissy-license-plate

Buc-ee's
https://www.buc-ees.com/index.php
https://www.houstonchronicle.com/news/
houston-texas/article/Buc-ee-s-is-a-beacon-
for-celebs-on-the-road-like-14283812.php#
https://www.texasmonthly.com/articles/
buc-ees-the-path-to-world-domination/
https://www.click2houston.com/
lifestyle/2019/09/24/buc-ees-is-no-1-texas-
chains-mega-gas-stations-have-highest-
rated-coffee-in-texas-us/
https://www.forbes.com/sites/
petercarbonara/2017/08/22/buc-ees-game-
of-porcelain-thrones/#1990ed537626

https://www.nytimes.com/2019/03/30/
style/bucees-texas.html

SLABs and Swangas
https://www.texasmonthly.com/the-
culture/slabs-donks-swangas-african-
american-car-club-seeks-home-changing-
austin/
https://www.texasmonthly.com/the-
culture/lil-keke-houston-celebrated-rapper-
started-career-car/
https://www.houstonchronicle.com/news/
houston-texas/houston/article/It-s-very-
special-What-it-takes-to-build-a-14045047.
php#
https://www.slabculture.com/about-us/
https://www.businessinsider.com/slabs-
swangas-custom-cars-houston-hip-hop-
culture-2019-5
https://www.youtube.com/watch?v=Brg__
M9YAL8
https://www.houstonchronicle.com/news/
houston-texas/houston/article/It-s-very-
special-What-it-takes-to-build-a-14045047.
php#
https://www.chron.com/entertainment/
article/houston-swangas-frozen-winter-
storm-reddit-2018-12507763.php#item-
85307-tbla-5
https://www.khou.com/article/news/verify-
is-there-a-restriction-on-how-far-rims-or-
swangas-can-stick-out/285-424d282d-0b27-
4b2b-8014-4450851a21a3
https://abc13.com/archive/7699639/

Pronunciation
https://www.nytimes.com/2017/01/26/
nyregion/houston-street-pronounce.html
https://abc13.com/traffic/how-do-
you-pronounce-these-houston-street-
names/4924822/
https://www.houstoniamag.com/news-and-
city-life/2013/06/whats-in-a-street-name-
may-2013
https://www.reddit.com/r/houston/
comments/7fnw2h/you_aint_from_
houston_unless_you_know_how_to/
https://www.reddit.com/r/houston/
comments/7fnw2h/you_aint_from_
houston_unless_you_know_how_to/
https://www.duchesne.org/admissions
https://communityimpact.com/austin/
news/2015/12/09/kuykendahl-road/
https://houstonhistorymagazine.org/
wp-content/uploads/2016/07/Germans-in-
Norhwest-Houston.pdf

You Need a Car

https://hogg.utexas.edu/wp-content/upload
s/2018/10/02C20W00120Houston20Area2
0Profile1.pdf
https://www.ridemetro.org/Pages/
Rail.aspx/posted/2491/METRORail_
SystemMap1_27_2010.468583.pdf
https://www.vice.com/en_us/
article/884kvk/why-the-us-sucks-at-
building-public-transit
https://www.vox.com/the-
goods/2018/12/7/18131132/public-
transportation-bus-subway-america-us
https://www.click2houston.com/
traffic/2019/09/06/a-look-at-houstons-
worst-commutes/

Freeway Nicknames

https://houstonnewcomerguides.com/
houston-highway-nicknames/
https://abc13.com/2991165/
https://www.click2houston.com/news/
local/2020/01/23/ask-2-why-do-houston-
freeways-have-multiple-names/
https://www.chron.com/news/houston-
texas/houston/article/A-transplant-s-guide-
to-the-names-of-Houston-s-13191043.php
https://www.houstonpublicmedia.
org/articles/news/
transportation/2015/09/03/213180/
understanding-the-nicknames-for-houston-
highways/
https://www.houstonpress.com/
news/a-drivers-guide-to-houstons-loop-
freeways-10721681
https://www.houstontx.gov/planning/
Demographics/Loop%2610%20Website/
https://www.mentalfloss.com/
article/67990/10-things-you-might-not-
know-about-us-interstate-system
Rodeo is a Really Big Deal
https://www.rodeohouston.com/About-Us/
Who-We-Are/Economic-Impact
https://annualreport.rodeohouston.com/
https://www.visithoustontexas.com/events/
livestock-show-and-rodeo/
https://www.click2houston.com/
rodeo/2020/03/11/houston-rodeo-
canceled-amid-growing-concerns-over-
coronavirus/
https://www.click2houston.com/
rodeo/2020/03/11/houston-rodeo-
canceled-amid-growing-concerns-over-
coronavirus/
https://www.click2houston.com/
rodeo/2020/03/02/here-are-the-maps-
for-the-2020-houston-livestock-show-and-
rodeo/

https://www.houstonpress.com/news/
the-houston-livestock-show-and-
rodeo-2020-11449300
https://www.rodeohouston.com/
News/Article/ArtMID/494/
ArticleID/2495/2019-A-Record-Breaking-
Year
https://annualreport.rodeohouston.com/
https://www.rodeohouston.com/Visit-the-
Rodeo/Rodeo/Super-Series
https://www.rodeohouston.com/visit-the-
rodeo/pre-rodeo-events/bar-b-que-contest
https://www.rodeohouston.com/Visit-the-
Rodeo/Livestock-Horse-Show/Livestock-
Show

Go Texan Day

https://tshaonline.org/handbook/online/
articles/hdh03
https://www.rodeohouston.com/Visit-the-
Rodeo/Pre-Rodeo-Events/Go-Texan-Day
https://www.republicbootcompany.com/
https://gomezwesternwear.net/men/
https://www.alshandmadeboots.com/
gallery.html
https://candelabootco.com/
https://www.pintoranch.com/

Trail Riders

https://www.rodeohouston.com/Visit-the-
Rodeo/Pre-Rodeo-Events/trail-rides
https://www.click2houston.com/
rodeo/2020/02/14/map-see-the-routes-of-
the-12-houston-rodeo-trail-rides/
https://www.houstonchronicle.com/news/
houston-texas/article/RodeoHouston-trail-
rides-2020-horses-on-highways-15083690.
php#photo-16975844
https://houstonhistorymagazine.org/
wp-content/uploads/2011/01/Trail-Rides-
Valdes.pdf
https://www.houstonpress.com/slideshow/
the-2020-houston-livestock-show-and-
rodeo-trail-riders-11452270
https://texashighways.com/culture/
history/historic-tales-from-the-largest-trail-
ride-in-the-world/
https://www.chron.com/news/houston-
texas/article/Houston-rodeo-Harris-
County-mounted-patrol-invites-15045184.
php
https://www.houstonpublicmedia.org/
articles/news/2017/03/02/190197/from-
the-border-to-houston-los-vaqueros-rio-
grande-ride-to-the-rodeo/

World's Greatest Bar-B-Que Competition

https://www.rodeohouston.com/visit-the-rodeo/pre-rodeo-events/bar-b-que-contest

https://www.click2houston.com/rodeo/2020/03/01/here-are-all-the-winners-of-the-houston-rodeo-2020-worlds-championship-bbq-contest/

https://www.chron.com/entertainment/restaurants-bars/bbq/article/RodeoHouston-s-barbecue-cook-off-results-15096651.php

https://www.khou.com/article/entertainment/events/rodeohouston/253-teams-to-compete-in-worlds-championship-bbq-contest-at-rodeohouston/285-e25c11d2-73f0-43a3-8deb-89e0767955b3

https://www.papercitymag.com/events/hlsr-bar-b-que-contest/

Carnival Food

https://www.rodeohouston.com/Visit-the-Rodeo/Attractions-Activities/Carnival

https://www.forbes.com/sites/loisaltermark/2018/05/30/how-thecreator-of-deep-fried-oreos-celebratesnational-doughnut-day/#574ae5806916

Street Art

https://houston.culturemap.com/news/arts/07-24-17-street-art-15-quintessential-houston-murals-instagram/#slide=0

https://www.houstoniamag.com/arts-and-culture/2018/06/houston-street-art-murals-instagram

https://houston.culturemap.com/news/arts/07-24-17-street-art-15-quintessential-houston-murals-instagram/#slide=0

https://carriecolbert.com/comprehensive-guide-houstons-colorful-walls/

https://www.visithoustontexas.com/things-to-do/arts-and-culture/visual-arts/murals-in-houston/

https://www.aerosolwarfare.com/

https://www.houstononthecheap.com/houston-murals-locations

https://www.houstonchronicle.com/news/houston-texas/houston/article/Street-artists-shine-at-Houston-mural-fest-14858187.php#

https://www.thegasamtexas.org/

https://abc13.com/be-someone-sign-houston-coronavirus-texas/5977560/

Art Car

https://www.houstonpress.com/news/2020-houston-art-car-parade-cancelled-11458630

https://www.houstonpress.com/arts/things-to-do-watch-the-houston-art-car-parade-in-downtown-11249425

https://www.thehoustonartcarparade.com/

https://www.thehoustonartcarparade.com/faq

https://www.thehoustonartcarparade.com/history-of-the-houston-art-car-para

http://dig.abclocal.go.com/ktrk/immersive/artcar/index.html

https://www.thehoustonartcarparade.com/grand-marshal

Mini Murals

http://minimurals.org/

http://minimurals.org/artists/

https://www.houstontx.gov/culturalaffairs/tsccartprogram.html

http://minimurals.org/houston/

Houston Theatre District

https://www.downtownhouston.org/district/theater/

https://www.visithoustontexas.com/theater/

https://www.theaterdistricthouston.org/

https://www.narcity.com/news/us/tx/houston/watch-houstons-alley-theatre-from-home-with-their-new-play

https://preview.houstonchronicle.com/art-exhibits/when-the-show-must-go-on-arts-groups-go-online-15138211

https://www.houstongrandopera.org/abouthgo

https://houstonsymphony.org/about-us/pressroom/media-kit/

https://www.visithoustontexas.com/theater/venues/jones-hall/

https://www.alleytheatre.org/about-us/rob-melrose

Houston's Rap Scene

https://www.houstonchronicle.com/entertainment/music/article/Meet-the-man-chronicling-Houston-s-hip-hop-13291328.php

https://utpress.utexas.edu/podcasts/lance-scott-walker-houston-rap-tapes

https://www.youtube.com/watch?v=rc33tuLIsNM

https://www.youtube.com/watch?v=zHn4w7fz80M

https://www.texasmonthly.com/articles/awesome-photos-of-houstons-rap-scene/

https://www.texasobserver.org/hip-hop-h-town/

https://www.vibe.com/2016/03/houston-rap-20-year-anniversary-scarface-ugk-dj-screw

https://www.npr.org/2019/06/10/731076691/bushwick-bill-of-houston-rap-group-geto-boys-dead-at-52

https://www.npr.org/2019/05/29/726615663/geto-boys-mind-playing-tricks-on-me-anxiety-american-anthem

https://www.latimes.com/entertainment/music/la-et-ms-bushwick-bill-20190610-story.html

https://www.npr.org/templates/story/story.php?storyId=7550286

https://www.chron.com/entertainment/article/Houston-featured-in-N-W-A-movie-6443303.php

https://www.kut.org/post/houston-rap-tapes-encyclopedic-look-bayou-citys-hip-hop-culture-and-history

http://www.peterbeste.com/houston/

https://www.npr.org/sections/therecord/2012/01/23/143799814/it-was-like-flies-to-honey-25-years-of-rap-a-lot-records

https://www.houstonpress.com/arts/nine-truths-cut-from-straight-outta-compton-the-nwa-movie-7681919

https://www.theguardian.com/music/2010/nov/11/dj-screw-drake-fever-ray

https://www.texasmonthly.com/articles/the-slow-life-and-fast-death-of-dj-screw/

https://www.independent.co.uk/arts-entertainment/music/bushwick-bill-dead-geto-boys-shot-self-eye-head-album-we-cant-be-stopped-a8952396.html

The Menil Collection

https://tshaonline.org/handbook/online/articles/klr01

https://www.menil.org/about

https://www.menil.org/campus

https://www.nytimes.com/1986/05/18/magazine/the-de-menil-family-the-medici-of-modern-art.html

https://www.menil.org/exhibitions/254-thirty-works-for-thirty-years

https://www.npr.org/sections/coronavirus-live-updates/2020/04/06/828506423/could-society-move-toward-normalcy-before-a-coronavirus-vaccine-is-ready

https://www.npr.org/2011/03/01/134160717/meditation-and-modern-art-meet-in-rothko-chapel

https://www.newyorker.com/magazine/2016/12/19/the-dark-final-years-of-mark-rothko

https://www.theguardian.com/artanddesign/2009/dec/12/mark-rothko-red-william-boyd

What Is a Bayou?

https://www.nationalgeographic.org/encyclopedia/bayou/

https://www.houstoniamag.com/news-and-city-life/2016/10/what-is-a-bayou-and-how-do-you-pronounce-it

https://www.chron.com/news/houston-texas/article/What-s-a-bayou-It-s-all-in-the-name-1809443.php

https://metro.co.uk/2017/08/30/what-is-a-bayou-hurricane-harvey-causes-the-american-waterways-to-overflow-6889414/

Bluebonnets

https://www.click2houston.com/news/local/2020/03/04/8-of-the-best-places-to-see-bluebonnets-in-the-houston-area/

https://www.khou.com/article/news/the-top-11-spots-in-the-houston-area-to-see-bluebonnets/285-20a7f9c7-f84c-4f2e-91c8-e3f4de3491b9

https://www.visithoustontexas.com/blog/post/houston-in-full-bloom-where-to-find-bluebonnets-in-and-around-houston/

https://aggie-horticulture.tamu.edu/archives/parsons/flowers/bluebonnet/bluebonnetstory.html

https://www.countryliving.com/gardening/g3117/bluebonnet-facts/

https://www.travelandleisure.com/trip-ideas/nature-travel/texas-bluebonnet-bloom-best-in-years

Grackles

https://houstonaudubon.org/birding/gallery/great-tailed-grackle.html

https://www.khou.com/article/life/animals/grackles-black-birds-houston/285-dd39c504-a12d-440b-b1ed-9f80b8e0c381

https://www.houstonpublicmedia.org/articles/shows/houston-matters/2018/12/12/315146/whats-the-deal-with-houstons-grackle-infestation/

https://www.chron.com/news/houston-texas/texas/article/Grackles-Texas-worst-bird-9200634.php#photo-10887602

https://www.allaboutbirds.org/guide/Great-tailed_Grackle/overview

https://www.houstonchronicle.com/local/gray-matters/article/Why-do-grackles-flock-to-parking-lots-at-dusk-7235072.php#

https://www.youtube.com/watch?v=8Mb9x0YwU3g

https://theleadernews.com/why-do-grackles-congregate/

https://www.texasmonthly.com/the-daily-post/eight-reasons-grackles-are-awesome/

https://nhpbs.org/wild/Icteridae.asp

Houston Arboretum

https://houstonarboretum.org/visit/plan-your-visit/discovery-room/

https://houstonarboretum.org/

https://www.visithoustontexas.com/listings/houston-arboretum-%26-nature-center/19602/

https://www.houstoniamag.com/travel-and-outdoors/2019/08/houston-arboretum-nature-center-renovation-2020

https://www.youtube.com/watch?v=lJhZCTuiOCI

https://blog.nwf.org/2015/01/10-nutty-facts-to-make-you-appreciate-squirrels/

Peacocks

https://www.houstonchronicle.com/local/gray-matters/article/Peacocks-gone-wild-5672212.php#

https://abc13.com/pets-animals/neighbors-have-love-hate-relationship-with-peacock-swarm/5399415/

https://www.click2houston.com/news/2017/09/28/peacocks-living-among-harvey-debris-in-west-houston/

https://baldheretic.com/2010/03/01/the-wild-peafowl-of-west-houston

https://www.texasstandard.org/stories/a-peacocks-tale-how-these-colorful-birds-came-to-be-in-texas/

https://www.chron.com/life/article/Peacocks-call-River-Forest-neighborhood-home-1792045.php

http://swamplot.com/where-the-peacocks-muster-near-hobby-airport/2017-01-11/

https://www.theatlantic.com/science/archive/2018/12/peacock-crests-are-vibration-sensors/578656/

Mosquitoes

https://www.smithsonianmag.com/science-nature/why-do-mosquitoes-bite-some-people-more-than-others-10255934/?page=9

https://www.houstontx.gov/health/NewsReleases/mosquito-bite-prevention.html

https://www.houstonchronicle.com/business/houston-how-to/article/Can-t-stand-mosquito-bites-Here-s-how-to-14381939.php

http://publichealth.harriscountytx.gov/Resources/Mosquito-Vector-Borne-Illnesses

https://www.youtube.com/watch?v=MnFnJddmWCM

https://www.foxnews.com/science/mosquitoes-orkin-cities-list

https://texasinsects.tamu.edu/mosquito/

https://www.houstontx.gov/health/Epidemiology/Informatics/documents/Mosquito.pdf

https://www.houstonchronicle.com/lifestyle/renew-houston/health/article/How-is-Houston-combatting-mosquitoes-13864834.php

https://natran.com/common-mosquitos-in-houston-and-when-to-seek-mosquito-control/

https://www.texasobserver.org/mosquitoes-are-bad-so-are-the-chemicals-some-texas-cities-are-using-to-kill-them/

https://www.chron.com/search/?action=search&searchindex=solr&query=mosquito+truck+spray&sort=date#mobile-filter-button

https://entomologytoday.org/2019/03/19/toxorhynchites-rutilus-mosquito-appetite-other-mosquitoes/

Bats

https://www.houstontx.gov/parks/batpage.html

https://houstonaudubon.org/programs/learn/bats.html

https://www.houstonchronicle.com/life/gardening/article/Texas-is-a-haven-for-31-species-of-bats-4812031.php

https://abc13.com/bats-houston-mammals-flying/2919478/

https://www.khou.com/article/news/local/upper-kirby-apartment-complex-infested-with-bats-lawsuit-claims/285-98bdc760-0df1-4a50-8ddc-5126d1191bf1

https://www.houstonzoo.org/explore/animals/bat-sebas-short-tailed/

https://www.houstoniamag.com/news-and-city-life/2018/03/waugh-bat-colony-after-harvey

https://www.southernliving.com/news/houston-bat-colony-office-building

https://www.houstonchronicle.com/opinion/outlook/article/Stop-blaming-bats-for-coronavirus-Opinion-15171316.php

https://tpwd.texas.gov/education/resources/keep-texas-wild/hanging-around-with-bats/a-year-in-the-life-of-a-mexican-free-tailed-bat

https://www.pwrc.usgs.gov/bioeco/mftbat.htm

https://www.nps.gov/ever/learn/nature/brazilianfreetailedbat.htm

https://statesymbolsusa.org/symbol-official-item/texas/state-mammal/mexican-free-tailed-bat

https://www.motherearthnews.com/nature-and-environment/control-insects-bolstering-bat-habitat-zmaz01aszsel

Friday Night Lights

https://www.houstontexans.com/kids/high-school-football

https://www.houstonchronicle.com/sports/highschool/article/Most-expensive-high-school-football-stadiums-Texas-13145194.php#photo-13663641

https://www.theguardian.com/sport/2017/aug/18/legacy-stadium-texas-high-school-football-katy

https://www.chron.com/neighborhood/katy/news/article/Cost-of-new-Katy-ISD-stadium-tops-70-million-10420748.php

https://www.maxpreps.com/rankings/football/1/state/texas.htm

https://www.chron.com/sports/highschool/article/Things-to-know-about-high-school-football-in-Texas-9193558.php

https://fanbuzz.com/high-school/berry-center-cy-fair-fcu-stadium/

https://www.houstonchronicle.com/sports/highschool/article/Most-expensive-high-school-football-stadiums-Texas-13145194.php#photo-10461156

https://bleacherreport.com/articles/2528561-the-state-of-high-school-football-recruiting-in-texas

https://www.chron.com/sports/texans/slideshow/Current-NFL-players-from-Houston-185136/photo-16477742.php

Galveston

https://tshaonline.org/handbook/online/articles/hdg01

https://www.houstoniamag.com/arts-and-culture/2018/12/dickens-on-the-strand

https://thedaytripper.com/daytrips/galveston-tx/

https://www.texasmonthly.com/the-culture/galveston-blue-water/

https://www.chron.com/opinion/king/article/Galveston-Bay-s-muddy-waters-solely-our-fault-5610001.php

http://www.pier21galveston.com/attractions/

https://www.moodygardens.com/attractions/

Maca, Kathleen Shanahan, *Ghosts of Galveston*

Cycling

https://www.houstoniamag.com/health-and-wellness/2015/07/riding-with-the-pack-a-guide-to-houstons-bike-clubs

https://bikehouston.org/rides/

https://www.criticalmasshouston.com/

https://www.spinlister.com/blog/houston-american-cycling-powerhouse/

https://www.click2houston.com/news/2019/04/27/more-than-9000-participants-kick-off-annual-bp-ms-150/

https://www.click2houston.com/community/2019/04/14/your-guide-to-the-annual-bp-ms-150-ride-to-austin/

https://houstonbikeplan.org/current-projects/

Soccer

https://www.houstondynamo.com/

https://www.houstondynamo.com/houstondash

https://www.gusleagues.com/soccer-home

https://www.houstonpublicmedia.org/articles/news/sports/2018/05/26/287778/houston-has-two-new-soccer-play-spaces/

https://abc13.com/houston-fc-soccer-college-high-school/5373277/

https://www.toroshtx.com/

Greenspace

https://www.houstontx.gov/parks/parksites/memorialpark.html

https://www.houstontx.gov/parks/parksites/index.html

http://www.greenhoustontx.gov/greenspace.html

https://buffalobayou.org/calendar/

http://www.pct3.com/Parks/terry-hershey-park

Museum District

https://houmuse.org/

https://www.visithoustontexas.com/listings/houston-museum-district/19642/

http://www.hmns.org/visit/about/

https://www.tripadvisor.com/AttractionsNear-g56003-d212138-Houston_Museum_District-Houston_Texas.html

NASA Love

https://spacecenter.org/exhibits-and-experiences/level-9-tour/

https://www.nasa.gov/press-release/nasa-s-newest-astronauts-ready-for-space-station-moon-and-mars-missions

https://www.space.com/spacex-axiom-space-launching-private-astronauts-in-2021.html

https://www.houstonchronicle.com/news/houston-texas/houston/article/Astronauts-the-true-experts-of-isolation-give-15151084.php#

https://communityimpact.com/houston/bay-area/government/2020/03/07/johnson-space-center-training-astronauts-for-missions-to-moon-mars/

https://www.houstonpublicmedia.
org/articles/shows/mockingbird-
armadillo/2019/06/28/338124/watch-
inside-the-astronauts-homes-mockingbird-
and-armadillo/

https://www.khou.com/article/
tech/science/aerospace/apollo-11/
splashdown-parties-and-celebrations-
nasa-astronauts-called-this-clear-lake-
neighborhood-home/285-52a72a1a-bb7e-
4eba-aafc-e5ae012ad639

https://www.houstonpress.com/
news/houston-101-neighborhood-of-
astronauts-6721772

https://www.nasa.gov/johnson/exploration

https://www.spacex.com/elon-musk

https://history.nasa.gov/sp4801-chapter10.
pdf

https://www.rice.edu/nasa

https://er.jsc.nasa.gov/seh/ricetalk.htm

Nutcracker Market

https://www.houstonballet.org/plan-your-
visit/seat-maps/

https://www.houstoniamag.com/
coronavirus/2020/03/houston-ballet-
spring-nutcracker-market-open-online

https://www.houstonballet.org/
globalassets/pdp/nutcracker/press-release/
press-release_the-nutcracker-2017.pdf

https://www.houstoniamag.com/arts-
and-culture/2019/12/houston-ballet-the-
nutcracker-2019-review

https://texashighways.com/events/
houston-ballets-nutcracker-market/

https://www.thegrand.com/2019-
nutcracker/

https://www.houstonballet.org/about/
nutcracker-market/explore/spring-
spectacular/

Miller Outdoor Theatre

https://www.milleroutdoortheatre.com/

https://www.houstontx.gov/events/miller.
html

https://www.hermannpark.org/poi/36/

https://www.houstonpublicmedia.
org/articles/shows/unwrap-your-
candies-now/2019/06/07/335822/
cissy-segall-davis-chats-about-all-things-
miller-outdoor-theatre-and-artist-felipe-
lopez-talks-about-his-exhibit-the-want-in-
my-nature/

https://tshaonline.org/handbook/online/
articles/klm08

https://www.milleroutdoortheatre.com/
past-and-present/

Freedom Over Texas

https://www.houstontx.gov/july4/

https://www.facebook.com/freedomovertx/

https://www.houstonoem.
org/2019freedomovertexas/

https://abc13.com/freedom-over-texas-july-
4-houston-fireworks-citgo/5297625/

https://www.houstonpress.com/music/a-
peek-behind-the-fireworks-curtain-of-
freedom-over-texas-8530909

https://www.papercitymag.com/culture/
houston-fourth-july-ultimate-guide-
fireworks-freedom-over-texas/

https://www.downtownhouston.org/
calendar/freedom-over-texas-fireworks-
presented-shell/2142/

https://www.thrillist.com/events/houston/
houston-4th-of-july-fireworks-2019

https://www.fox26houston.com/news/
houston-celebrates-independence-day-at-
freedom-over-texas

https://www.houstonpress.com/news/
rainy-weather-flooding-shuts-down-citgo-
freedom-over-texas-10630182

https://www.southernliving.com/travel/
where-to-watch-fireworks-houston

https://www.houstontx.gov/july4/faq.html

https://www.houstontx.gov/july4/stages.
html

Beer Can House

https://www.orangeshow.org/beer-can-
house

https://www.orangeshow.org/beer-can-
house-history

https://www.visithoustontexas.com/
listings/the-beer-can-house/20293/

https://houston.culturemap.com/guide/
entertainment/beer-can-house/

https://www.dailymail.co.uk/news/
article-2380661/Texas-Beer-house-50-000-
cans-unusual-tourist-attractions-Houston.
html

National Museum of Funeral History

https://www.nmfh.org/exhibits/permanent-
exhibits/bush-memorial-exhibit

https://www.houstonchronicle.com/
entertainment/theater/article/Icons-in-Ash-
at-the-National-Museum-of-14281182.php#

https://www.chron.com/neighborhood/
champions-klein/business/article/Funeral-
history-museum-focuses-on-the-beauty-
and-14568668.php

https://investors.sci-corp.com/

Last Concert Cafe

https://www.lastconcert.com/?tribe-bar-date=2020-02

https://www.facebook.com/thelastconcertcafe/

https://www.downtownhouston.org/guidedetail/bars-clubs/last-concert-cafe/

https://www.houstonpress.com/location/last-concert-cafe-6784712

https://www.houstonchronicle.com/entertainment/restaurants-bars/article/New-partners-invest-in-upgrading-Houston-s-Last-13804876.php

https://www.houstonchronicle.com/entertainment/music/article/Say-hello-to-Houston-s-newest-and-oldest-13810067.php

https://houston.culturemap.com/news/real-estate/07-12-11-always-a-classic-last-concert-cafe-is-now-a-historic-landmark-former-speakeasy-gets-protected-status/

https://www.houstoniamag.com/editors-note/2016/10/editors-note-last-concert-cafe-hidden-houston

https://www.chron.com/neighborhood/article/Elusive-Last-Concert-Cafe-exudes-warmth-9578427.php

https://www.houstontx.gov/planning/HistoricPres/landmarks/11PL99_Last_Concert_Cafe_1403_Nance_St.pdf

La Carafe

https://www.owlnet.rice.edu/~hans320/projects/lacarafe/building.html

https://www.chron.com/chrontv/this-forgotten-day-in-houstonredesign1/article/La-Carafe-Houston-s-oldest-haunted-bar-6831418.php

https://abc13.com/localish/inside-the-most-haunted-bar-in-houston/5661655/

https://www.click2houston.com/houston-life/2019/12/10/grab-a-cold-beer-at-one-of-houstons-oldest-bars/

https://www.houstonchronicle.com/life/article/La-Carafe-is-rich-with-Texas-history-3717510.php

https://houston.culturemap.com/guide/bars/la-carafe/

Mattress Mack

https://www.galleryfurniture.com/give-back-to-the-community.html

https://www.galleryfurniture.com/customer-service/policies/company-history.html

https://www.chron.com/news/houston-texas/slideshow/10-things-you-may-not-know-about-Jim-McIngvale-55007/photo-4017672.php

https://www.galleryfurniture.com/customer-service/policies/mattress-mack.html

https://www.houstonchronicle.com/texas-sports-nation/astros/article/Mattress-Mack-s-13-million-bets-on-Astros-to-win-14703568.php#

https://abc13.com/mattress-mack-birthday-things-we-love-about-to-know/3057364/

https://www.houstonchronicle.com/business/article/Forbes-tally-shows-fortunes-rise-for-Houston-13665718.php

https://www.facebook.com/mattressmack/posts/here-is-the-transcript-for-a-speech-i-gave-in-april-at-the-2013-aaf-houston-and-/635747513111431/

H-E-B

https://careers.heb.com/about-h-e-b/

https://www.kut.org/post/why-texans-love-h-e-b-so-much

https://www.click2houston.com/features/2020/03/15/what-we-love-about-texas-how-h-e-b-has-become-such-a-thing-for-texans/

https://www.statesman.com/NEWS/20161012/25-reasons-why-Texans-so-rightfully-love-H-E-B

https://tshaonline.org/handbook/online/articles/dhh01

https://www.texasmonthly.com/the-daily-post/heb-took-care-communities-harvey/

https://www.heb.com/static-page/article-template/Our-History

J. J. Watt

https://bleacherreport.com/articles/2881122-report-jj-watt-wife-kealia-donate-350k-to-houston-food-bank-amid-coronavirus

http://jjwfoundation.org/the-foundation/

https://www.si.com/nfl/2019/08/29/texans-jj-watt-hurricane-harvey-funds-homes-built-meals-houston

https://www.chron.com/sports/texans/article/Texans-JJ-Watt-Kealia-Ohai-donate-350K-Food-Bank-15133048.php

https://abc13.com/sh-99-jj-watt-parkway-grand-hurricane-harvey/2371271/

http://www.nfl.com/player/j.j.watt/2495488/profile

https://www.houstonchronicle.com/texas-sports-nation/brian-t-smith/article/J-J-Watt-Texans-lifetime-career-15190751.php?utm_source=twitter.com&utm_medium=referral&utm_campaign=sftwitter#

https://www.foxsports.com/nfl/gallery/22-things-you-might-not-have-known-about-j-j-watt-101814

AstroWorld https://tshaonline.org/handbook/online/articles/lsa01
https://www.houstoniamag.com/news-and-city-life/2018/05/astroworld
https://www.houstonpress.com/arts/its-been-50-years-since-astroworld-opened-its-doors-in-houston-10495775
https://scholarworks.sfasu.edu/cgi/viewcontent.cgi?article=1922&context=ethj
https://houston.culturemap.com/news/real-estate/12-15-12-astroworld-site-sold-for-428-million-rodeo-unsure-of-plans-for-hallowed-amusement-park-land/#slide=0
https://www.houstonchronicle.com/business/article/Jury-Investors-taken-for-a-ride-11254691.php
http://swamplot.com/tag/astroworld/
https://houstonlibrary.org/learn-explore/exhibits/astroworld-model
https://www.texasmonthly.com/the-daily-post/houston-needs-another-astroworld/
https://www.papercitymag.com/real-estate/roy-hofheinz-private-penthouse-celestial-suite-astrodome-hotel-peek-inside/
https://www.amazon.com/Astrodomain-Astrodome-Astroworld-Hotels-Astrohall/dp/B00161WH4O
https://sixflags.fandom.com/wiki/Showcase_Theatre_(Six_Flags_AstroWorld)

Beyoncé
https://www.theguardian.com/music/2020/apr/24/beyonce-gives-6m-dollars-to-coronavirus-relief-mental-health-jack-dorsey
https://www.beyonce.com/beygoodhouston/
https://www.biography.com/musician/beyonce-knowles
https://www.businessinsider.com/beyonce-net-worth-fortune-spending-2018-8
https://www.essence.com/lifestyle/travel/how-to-spend-a-beyonce-themed-weekend-in-houston/
https://www.inc.com/peter-economy/17-of-most-inspirational-quotes-from-beyonce-business-genius-music-superstar.html
https://www.prnewswire.com/news-releases/beyonce-announces-the-formation-world-tour-300216392.html

Juan Carlos
https://www.houstoniamag.com/arts-and-culture/2014/06/the-montrose-rollerblade-dancer-goes-national-june-2014

https://www.reddit.com/r/houston/comments/bomxf8/where_has_juan_carlos_been_montrose_dancing/
https://www.houstonpublicmedia.org/articles/shows/houston-matters/2015/09/21/213347/juan-carlos-the-rollerblading-dancer-a-star-is-born-on-a-houston-street-corner/
https://www.dailydot.com/unclick/rollerblader-juan-carlos-tiktok/
https://www.houstonchronicle.com/life/article/A-star-is-born-at-the-corner-of-Montrose-and-5600283.php#
https://www.houstonchronicle.com/news/houston-texas/houston/article/Houston-Reality-TV-stars-14501754.php
https://www.houstoniamag.com/news-and-city-life/2013/09/wheels-of-fortune-september-2013

Astrodome
https://www.khou.com/article/news/local/105-million-astrodome-makeover-approved-by-county-commissioners/285-518047861
https://tshaonline.org/handbook/online/articles/xva01
https://www.houstonchronicle.com/news/houston-texas/houston/article/What-s-going-on-with-the-Astrodome-Nothing-14423650.php#
https://www.theatlantic.com/entertainment/archive/2013/11/the-sad-fate-but-historic-legacy-of-the-houston-astrodome/281269/
https://www.bizjournals.com/houston/news/2013/12/31/year-in-review-astrodome.html
https://www.astroturf.com/about-synthetic-turf/astroturf-history/
https://www.sbnation.com/lookit/2017/10/15/16478414/astros-astrodome-groundbreaking-guns-photo-1962-mlb
https://www.ktre.com/2020/04/09/way-back-sports-houston-astrodome-opened-april/

The Bush Family
https://www.houstonchronicle.com/news/houston-texas/houston/article/A-Statesman-Remembered-12861590.php
https://www.chron.com/news/houston-texas/texas/article/When-and-why-did-the-Bush-family-move-to-Texas-12844094.php
https://www.fly2houston.com/iah/overview/

https://www.youtube.com/watch?v=8HLATbmi3gU

https://en.wikipedia.org/wiki/West_Oaks,_Houston

https://www.houstonchronicle.com/news/houston-texas/houston/article/George-H-W-Bush-s-Houston-office-closes-up-13727934.php

https://www.downtownhouston.org/guidedetail/sights-attractions/george-bush-monument/

https://www.wsj.com/articles/in-houston-his-adopted-home-george-h-w-bush-was-beloved-1543720359

https://www.nytimes.com/2018/12/01/us/george-bush-houston.html

https://abc13.com/society/how-the-bushes-chose-houston-as-a-home/3358861/

https://www.reuters.com/article/us-people-bush-houston/houston-residents-by-the-thousands-mourn-president-george-hw-bush-idUSKBN1O52AQ

https://abc13.com/george-hw-bush-death-died-dead-barbara/4805178/

https://www.houstonchronicle.com/life/features/article/George-H-W-Bush-and-a-legacy-of-philanthropy-13448301.php

https://abcnews.go.com/US/back-george-hw-bushs-colorful-history-fun-socks/story?id=59574889

Sam Houston

https://tshaonline.org/handbook/online/articles/fho73

https://www.history.com/topics/mexico/sam-houston

https://www.history.com/news/7-things-you-may-not-know-about-sam-houston

https://www.pbs.org/weta/thewest/people/d_h/houston.htm

https://www.britannica.com/biography/Sam-Houston

https://www.biography.com/political-figure/sam-houston

https://www.theatlantic.com/politics/archive/2011/04/picture-of-the-day-the-battle-of-san-jacinto-175-years-ago-today/237669/

https://tshaonline.org/handbook/online/articles/fho73

https://www.sanjacinto-museum.org/The_Battle/Commanders/Santa_Anna/#Pane2

Marvin Zindler

https://tshaonline.org/handbook/online/articles/fzind

http://dig.abclocal.go.com/ktrk/immersive/marvin-zindler/index.html

https://www.nytimes.com/2007/08/02/us/02zindler.html

https://www.texasmonthly.com/articles/marvin-zindler-consumer-lawman/

https://www.chron.com/news/houston-texas/article/Channel-13-s-Marvin-Zindler-dies-at-85-1632658.php

https://abc13.com/food/eado-restaurant-names-burger-after-abc13s-marvin-zindler/5868372/

https://tshaonline.org/handbook/online/articles/ysc01

Red Duke, MD

https://www.tmc.edu/news/2019/03/im-dr-red-duke/#single-article-body

http://www.memorialhermann.org/rememberingred/

https://www.houstonpublicmedia.org/articles/shows/houston-matters/2018/10/04/306677/biography-remembers-houstons-beloved-cowboy-doctor/?utm_source=rss-houston-matters-article&utm_medium=link&utm_campaign=hpm-rss-link

https://www.houstonchronicle.com/news/health/article/Iconic-Houston-surgeon-Dr-Red-Duke-dies-6465619.php#

http://www.memorialhermann.org/our-dr-duke-stories/#mentor

https://corps.tamu.edu/dr-james-h-red-duke-jr-50/

https://houston.culturemap.com/news/city-life/12-10-18-dr-red-duke-ut-hermann-biography-im-red-duke-bryant-boutwell-life-flight/

https://www.houstoniamag.com/news-and-city-life/2015/11/how-doctor-red-duke-saved-my-dad-december-2015

https://www.tmc.edu/news/2019/03/im-dr-red-duke/

https://trauma.memorialhermann.org/rememberingred/

https://tshaonline.org/handbook/online/articles/fduke

https://www.faa.gov/documentLibrary/media/Order/7340.2F_Chg_1_dtd_2-4-16.pdf

Cost of Living

https://www.bestplaces.net/cost_of_living/city/texas/houston

https://economics21.org/is-houston-really-less-affordable-than-new-york

https://www.texasmonthly.com/news/houston-affordability-transportation-costs/

https://houston.innovationmap.com/
houston-best-home-value-us-affordability-
the-zebra-real-estate-for-sale-2645409046.
html

https://www.zillow.com/houston-tx/home-
values/

https://www.expatistan.com/cost-of-living/
houston

Air-Conditioning

https://www.theatlantic.com/technology/
archive/2011/07/keepin-it-cool-how-
the-air-conditioner-made-modern-
america/241892/

https://www.click2houston.com/houston-
life/2020/02/25/houston-history-the-first-
high-rise-in-houston-built-with-central-air-
conditioning/

https://www.chron.com/life/gray/article/
Gray-Air-conditioning-capital-of-the-
world-3653254.php

https://www.texasmonthly.com/articles/
the-hottest-place-in-the-whole-u-s-a/

Basements

https://dengarden.com/basements/Why-
Dont-Homes-in-Texas-Have-Basements

https://www.texasmonthly.com/being-
texan/texanist-dont-texas-houses-
basements/

https://www.southernliving.com/home/
texas-homes-no-basements

https://www.chron.com/neighborhood/
bellaire/news/article/Once-and-for-all-
West-U-council-approves-9330093.php

https://www.hammerpedia.com/frost-line-
map/

INDEX